FOUR LAST SONGS

FOUR LAST SONGS

Aging and Creativity in Verdi, Strauss, Messiaen, and Britten

LINDA HUTCHEON AND MICHAEL HUTCHEON

THE UNIVERSITY OF CHICAGO PRESS

CHICAGO AND LONDON

LINDA HUTCHEON is university professor emeritus of English and comparative literature at the University of Toronto. MICHAEL HUTCHEON is a pulmonologist and professor of medicine at the University of Toronto.

The University of Chicago Press, Chicago 60637
The University of Chicago Press, Ltd., London
© 2015 by The University of Chicago
All rights reserved. Published 2015.
Printed in the United States of America

24 23 22 21 20 19 18 17 16 15   2 3 4 5

ISBN-13: 978-0-226-25559-0 (cloth)
ISBN-13: 978-0-226-25562-0 (e-book)
DOI: 10.7208/chicago/9780226255620.001.0001

Library of Congress Cataloging-in-Publication Data

Hutcheon, Linda, 1947– author.
  Four last songs : aging and creativity in Verdi, Strauss, Messiaen, and Britten / Linda Hutcheon, Michael Hutcheon.
    pages cm
  Includes bibliographical references and index.
  ISBN 978-0-226-25559-0 (cloth : alkaline paper)—ISBN 0-226-25559-x (cloth : alkaline paper)—ISBN 978-0-226-25562-0 (e-book)—ISBN 0-226-25562-x (e-book)
  1. Composers—Biography. 2. Britten, Benjamin, 1913–1976—Last years.
  3. Messiaen, Olivier, 1908–1992—Last years. 4. Strauss, Richard, 1864–1949—Last years. 5. Verdi, Giuseppe, 1813–1901—Last years. 6. Aging—Psychological aspects. 7. Creative ability in old age. I. Hutcheon, Michael, 1945– author.
  II. Title.
  ML390.H877 2015
  780.92'2—dc23

                                                          2014036323

⊚ This paper meets the requirements of ANSI/NISO Z39.48-1992 (Permanence of Paper).

What claims to wisdom can age authorize in a culture increasingly de-mocratized by its own technological powers, so that the young may appear to be more adaptive than the old, and the sense of history seem more a burden than a source of access to sustaining truths about a common human condition?
—Murray M. Schwarz, introduction to *Memory and Desire: Aging—Literature—Psychoanalysis*

Age can do less and less, but age continues to know, indeed knows more and more, grows more and more in understanding, in the strong wisdom of the heart, and that is what makes the cruel and beautiful paradox of age.
—Norman N. Holland, "Not So Little Hans: Identity and Aging"

CONTENTS

CHAPTER ONE

Setting the Stage

S everal years ago, on a visit to the Cloisters of the Metropolitan Museum of Art in New York City, we came upon an early sixteenth-century tapestry from the Southern Lowlands called "The Hunt of the Frail Stag" (fig. 1). Here the stag, which represents humanity, is pursued by passions, sickness, old age, and death. In one of these allegorical fragments, the stag is driven from a lake by a huntress (Old Age) and her hounds. A text on a banner informs us (translated from the Old French):

> Then Old Age mounts an all-out assault
> That drives him from the lake
> And unleashes upon him Pain and Doubt,
> Cold and Heat, and thus brings on
> Care and Trouble to seize him.
> And Age with wrinkled flesh
> And Heaviness make him flee
> Toward Sickness, the dreaded one.[1]

Clearly, we decided, this was proof that age and its trials have concerned artists ever since enough people survived into their later years to contemplate the issue. Our response to this image was a complex one, however. We recognized in it an undercurrent of concern, not to say dread, about aging that is prevalent in our own times—witness the ubiquitous rueful jokes about memory or physical changes associated with age. But, thanks to the examples of family and friends, we also knew well the possibility of full and fulfilling later lives. This allegorical tapestry evoked in us an appreciation of one of the many dichotomies of aging: a sense of worry, even fear, on one hand, matched by the prospect of a contented older age, on the

Fig. 1. Old Age Drives the Stag out of a Lake and the Hounds Heat, Grief, Cold, Anxiety, Age, and Heaviness Pursue Him (from *The Hunt of the Frail Stag*). Image copyright © The Metropolitan Museum of Art. Image source: Art Resource, NY

other. How did these divergent responses come to coexist? We asked ourselves the obvious question: how should we think about our aging selves and our futures?

As we entered our sixties, it occurred to us that there were few models for what is essentially a new period of life beyond what has been, for a century, the usual time of retirement. Recent ways of thinking about later life were unappealing to us: for example, both midlife styles (where we simply continue to do what we have always done) and the multiple roles postulated in what is being called "postmodern" aging (as defined in terms of a specifically consumer culture). Because continuing creativity in older age is an important value for us, we decided to examine the lives of members of earlier generations, specifically (given our interests) composers, in order to understand the role that their later years played in the context of their entire artistic life course. In the process we have ranged widely in our reading from the many dimensions that comprise gerontology through to the various disciplines of the humanities. This range reflects our belief that understanding creativity and aging demands multiple perspectives on everything from biography to identity, history to aesthetics, politics to social and cultural value.

This, then, is a book about aging and creativity. We realize that these two words do not always go together in most people's minds. As Kathleen Woodward pointedly puts it, "Neither in Freudian analysis nor in other major discourses of western culture do we find old age represented . . . in terms of new forms of creativity in later life."[2] However, the lives of such artists as Michelangelo (1475–1564), Goethe (1749–1832), and Elliott Carter (1908–2012) attest that creativity and later life are by no means mutually exclusive. Much fine scholarly work has been done on the last works of visual artists, writers, and composers. *Four Last Songs* (with its obvious reference to the late orchestral lieder of Richard Strauss) offers a series of case studies of the last works and late careers of four composers who led long creative lives. They are all canonical figures: Giuseppe Verdi (1813–1901) (with the inevitable presence of Richard Wagner [1813–1883]), Richard Strauss (1864–1949), Olivier Messiaen (1908–1992), and Benjamin Britten (1913–1976). In each case the composers' own attitudes to their aging and their creativity, the works of their late years, and the reception of those final works form part of our focus.

As a literary theorist and a physician, we have previously used opera as the cultural vehicle and focus of three coauthored books.[3] Here once again we have turned to music and particularly opera, but this time it is in order to study not disease, the body, or death, but rather the intersection of aging and creativity in Western European culture of the last two centuries. Opera is an art form with a four-hundred-year continuous history, a complex form that brings together (even before its staged production) multiple arts: music, drama, and poetry. But because it is a staged as well as a complex dramatic form, it is by definition an expensive art form to produce. Therefore its creators have always been compelled to seek out topics of wide and powerful appeal—playing to not only the desires of their audiences, but their anxieties as well. Therefore, from its origins in Renaissance Italy, opera has, famously and not surprisingly, explored themes of concern to most people's lives, then and now: love (in all its tragic and comic consequences) and death (and, along with it, both grief/loss and redemption). These central themes, combined with opera's visceral intensity as a staged art form, help explain its ongoing popularity and suggest a continuity of human concern that transcends time and place. However, as we shall see, history and culture do intervene in opera's treatment of the human universal of aging.

This is not really a book about how to age well, though its case studies might indeed offer some exemplars: all these composers were successful creative artists and very public figures, not to say national icons, in their respective countries (Italy, Germany, France, and Great Britain). Our primary interest here is in the intersection of aging and creativity, and we have chosen to study aging composers who wrote at least one major opera at the end of their lives. The commitment of time and creative energy required to compose such a long, complex, and public musical work inevitably left exposed and sometimes even threatened the creative (and psychic) resources of Verdi, Strauss, Messiaen, and Britten in different ways. Another reason for choosing composers who wrote operas late in life is that with that particular art form they had at their disposal a double means of expression—words *and* music. As a musical genre, opera is "texted"—that is, as we have seen, there is a dramatic story in words and actions as well as music to consider. It was the practice of each of these composers not only to compose the music, but also either to write the narrative of the libretto himself or to influence the story's development in major ways. The combined use of words and music opened channels of adaptation, self-expression, and perhaps even catharsis, all with the potential to help them explore their own aging and mortality in a creative way. Yet they too had to face challenges that came with their age, as well as their times—times that were changing socially, politically, and aesthetically, as of course all times do. But cultural eras bring specific challenges that are shared by those who live through them. Verdi and Wagner were of the same age cohort; later, so too were Messiaen and Britten; Strauss straddled the middle.

We have chosen nineteenth- and twentieth-century composers for a number of reasons. In this period they had much more control over their choice of both subject matter and style of musical composition than did court (or even commercial) composers of earlier times. Also, by then the composer had superseded both the librettist and the singer as the central artistic figure in operatic production. But another important reason is that the late nineteenth century also saw the discovery and definition of old age as a social, economic, and medical construct. And thus were born, in the twentieth century, both geriatrics and gerontology as disciplines.[4] From the nineteenth to the twenty-first centuries, medical advances and increased life expectancy have meant that a new period of later life has come into being for an increasing number of people, one as long as or, for some, longer than childhood. But it has been much less explored by theorists. In fact, you could say that an entire new generation has now been added to the life course.[5] There has been an increase in the absolute numbers of older individuals and also an increase in this group as a percentage of the total population. Finally, this aging population is itself aging: its average age is increasing as people live longer.[6] This book focuses primarily on what has been called the "Third Age"—that new period in later life in which older people remain independent, active, and capable; it will also, however, deal with the adaptations required by the next, the "Fourth Age" of increasing dependency and entry into "old old age,"[7] often caused by a break that signals "the irreversible exclusion of normal life, thus the end of normal life."[8] For some people, this may be what is feared even more than death itself.

The remainder of this introductory and orienting chapter will outline some of the basic issues and perspectives that underpin those that follow, with their stories of particular composers and their creative lives: the paradoxical cultural views of age and aging, the historical construction of the concept of "old age," and the notion of the composer's personhood and the role in it of creativity.

THE DICHOTOMIES OF AGING

Later life is a fraught topic in our current culture, with its commercialized, antiaging, death-denying ethos that aims to keep everyone young forever.[9] But the aging population today is paradoxically represented as both a privileged, wealthy cohort and a "gray tsunami" of future debt, debility, and health-care crises.[10] The fact is that at the end of the twentieth century, we saw "the simultaneous survival of the largest number of fit people in their sixties and seventies ever known, and of the largest numbers of chronically ill older people ever known."[11] From the scholarship across the disciplines on this topic, however, we can see that the elderly—across all times and places—have always been considered both rich and poor; they have been both venerated and denigrated; they have been treated both kindly and harshly in their families and communities. In many cultures they have been represented as both wise and foolish, as both powerful authorities and infirm burdens.

There is something about aging that generates this polarization of viewpoints, which may reflect our society's ambivalent attitudes: people want to live longer, but they don't want to age. In the twenty-first century, it has become almost a moral imperative to live as long as possible; but in our youth-oriented culture, no one wants to be "old," or, perhaps more to the point, to be seen as old. While much has been written about the limitations that come with aging, arguably many things can be gained for those who are fortunate enough to live into a "ripe" old age with the experience and knowledge that accompany the years.[12] Aging can be—and is—experienced in many different ways, but it is likely to bring changes that are physical, social, psychological, and sometimes cognitive. With changes come challenges to which we must all respond. Our ability to adapt to these alterations will determine how fulfilled we are in our later years. Indeed, these can be years not of stasis or decline, but of development. They can yield the polarities of either isolation and insularity or what has been called generativity,[13] with the elderly becoming teachers of the young, seeing their pedagogical task as one of conserving, passing on, and perhaps even leading forward. Even if their aim in doing so is to define and create their personal legacy, generativity is always also a commitment to the next generation.

Yet the most widely held view of aging in relation to creativity in particular is a rather different one, articulated most influentially by Kenneth Clark in his 1970 Rede Lecture, *The Artist Grows Old*. From this perspective, old-age creativity is characterized by a "sense of isolation, a feeling of holy rage, developing into . . . transcendental pessimism; a mistrust of reason, a belief in instinct."[14] Nevertheless, the critical literature in all the arts offers us multiple examples of major exceptions to this "rule" of intransigent elder rage and depression:[15] those artists blessed with serenity, resignation, contemplation, enhanced powers of intellect and understanding, and the play of accumulated knowledge and experience that are also said to come with age.[16]

Edward W. Said, in his posthumously published *On Late Style*, joined Clark in seeing as important only the unreconciled impatience that comes with older artists' feeling of imminent mortality: "But what of artistic lateness not as harmony and resolution but as intransigence, difficulty, and unresolved contradiction? What if age and ill health don't produce the serenity of 'ripeness is all'?"[17] For an artist at any age, the approach of death can add a new restlessness and urgency, a sense of unfinished business; but with increasing age, it becomes clearer that time is no longer "an inexhaustible commodity."[18] The awareness of the impending end can thus be a catalyst for creativity, the opportunity for epiphany and metaphysical transcendence.[19] What has been called the "swan-song phenomenon," as a means of coping with mortality, is what makes some creative artists concentrate on producing masterworks that will act as their final aesthetic legacy.[20] Yet, not surprisingly, there is the parallel dichotomous view, most famously articulated by Simone de Beauvoir, that age and mortality have only a negative effect on creativity, reducing strength and deadening emotion.[21] But what about creative artists who at the end of their lives, freed from public responsibility and expectations, claim to work only for their own pleasure? These are some of the many contrasting, often contradictory poles of opinion that have come to constitute Western culture's view of aging, especially in relation to creativity.

THE YOUNG HISTORY OF "OLD AGE"

The four composers we study here all lived in a modern Western culture that has become not only increasingly youth-oriented but also arguably gerontophobic, in the double meaning of the word: fear of growing old and fear of the elderly. This dual negative can be witnessed in society's frequent devaluing of its older members, in its marking of them in mostly pejorative terms: physical degeneration, mental decline, moral failings, poverty and dependency, and lack of productivity. There is a long history of this denigration, coming to a head in the late nineteenth century, where our examples begin.[22] What Margaret Gullette calls our culture's "decline narrative" was not always the dominant view of aging, of course.[23] While the fact of getting older may be a universal (for the fortunate), its meaning is culturally determined. The "Golden Age" theory (which some feel is really a myth) argues that in preindustrial Europe, adulthood flowed into old age with minimal differentiation: economic activities were part of family life, and no one ever "retired" from them.[24] According to this view, with the Industrial Revolution, urbanization, and the decline of the extended family, older people (specifically, those who were no longer capable of being productive workers) were displaced into poorhouses, hospitals, and then what were once called old-age homes. Suddenly they were seen—by everyone from efficiency experts in factories to reformers[25]—as a social and economic problem demanding a social response. The next century saw governments offer institutional solutions, including the establishing of pensions, in effect creating the very concept of retirement from employment. For many, mandatory retirement became one of the institutional causes of the increased segregation and thus the reduction in social status of older people.[26]

What Stephen Katz analyzes in depth as this "problematizing" of old age took another turn after World War II,[27] when a "functionalist" social theory came to dominate. Given that people were expected to inhabit roles that would support society's needs, older individuals presented a problem if they could no longer function in these roles. For this first-generation sociological theory,[28] "disengagement" was thus proposed as a normal adjustment, appropriate to the accommodation of declining health, energy, or capability.[29] Older individuals were to relinquish their usual social roles and "disengage"—thus easing their life in their later years. This view was subsequently dismissed by many as ageist in its marginalizing of the older population. However, this ethos of elderly passivity and lack of agency has to some extent persisted. Newer theories have attempted to counter it: "activity theory," for instance, suggested that older people take on new roles as they surrender former ones, remaining active and socially engaged.[30] While this sounds more positive, it too has come under attack: "the new old age is besieged by theorists, marketeers, and the media, who advocate an ethic of activity, whether in the form of social participation, education, volunteerism, or recreation. This, in turn, has contributed to new normative stereotypes also conveying an impoverished social meaning of aging and old age."[31] In response, a theory of "gerotranscendence" has been offered to describe a developmental pattern of positive aging that goes beyond the old dualism of activity and disengagement.[32] And there will undoubtedly be many other theories in the future.

Theories of aging and creativity, in particular, have developed in parallel with these more general sociological ones. One influential school of gerontological thought started in the nineteenth century with George Beard and Adolphe Quételet and was followed up in 1953 by Harvey Lehman in his influential book *Age and Achievement*. It argued (often from numerical data) that the last years of a creative artist's life—across the arts—are the least productive and the least innovative, and therefore the least creative.[33] Opera composers' peak productive years, for example, are said to be their forties, with a severe decline in later years.[34] Most of the arguments against this position have been made in the name of proving that older people can be and in fact are productive, rather than questioning the necessary correlation of creativity and productivity. After all, it is only since the Industrial Revolution that we have come to value individuals based on their productivity.[35] As we shall see, Benjamin Britten certainly composed fewer and shorter works than usual in his last years, after a disabling stroke, but the critics are unanimous in seeing in them both continuing imagination and the same command of his craft of composition. In fact, what Britten did was adapt to these challenges: while his productivity decreased, his creativity remained intact.

For creative artists in their later years, to internalize any part of their culture's negative views of aging can mean yet another kind of challenge—an aesthetic challenge to the value of their work and thus their artistic legacy. That familiar decline narrative of age is doubly threatening to creative artists: they have to come to terms not only with their own impending mortality but also with the fact that their audiences and critics will perceive them and their work differently as they age. Thus, late works are inevitably highly charged for artists as they contemplate the image of themselves and their work that they will leave behind. Expectations are high. The potential for failure hangs over them, and thus the possibility of permanent damage to their reputations as artists. On the other hand, a successful outcome may guarantee fame and lasting influence in the future and a new sense of personal fulfillment in the present. However, these last works are often received by their audiences differently from those that preceded them—as everything from the "last gasp" to the "opus ultimum."[36] Those dichotomies of aging persist. But, as we shall show in the chapters to follow, the composers we study not only faced this aesthetic challenge of reception but also dealt with it, as with all the other challenges of aging, each in his own individual way.

CREATIVE ARTISTS AS "PERSONS"

It is what we want to call their individual sense of "personhood" that is tested and at times even endangered by these challenges.[37] In his medical examination of the nature of suffering, Eric Cassell usefully (and rather expansively) describes a "person" as having "personality and character, a lived past, a family, a family's lived past, culture and society, roles, associations with others, a political dimension, activities, day-to-day behaviors, an existence below awareness, a body, a secret life, a believed-in future, and a transcendent dimension."[38] Each of these facets of personhood is susceptible to threat, which (depending on its intensity) can lead to stress, unhappiness, depression, or ultimately what Cassell calls suffering. Such a state may continue until the threat has passed or until the person's sense of "wholeness" has been restored through resiliency and growth or through Cassell's concept of "meaning and transcendence."[39] For a creative artist, creativity can potentially be involved in both the threat to personhood and the restoration: an overextension of one's creative resources can be threatening to personhood, just as validation through successful new creation can be restorative. While Cassell is not concerned with aging or with artists in particular, we most definitely are: for the composers we study, many of those facets of personhood were inseparable—positively or negatively—from their creativity as they aged. While all were open to threat, they were also open to potential enhancement. As Cassell says, persons "do things," and "if they cannot do the things they identify with the fact of their being, they are not whole."[40] Artists are, by definition, creative agents, and their creative agency may form a large part of their identity.

It is obvious that we can never know another's personhood completely—perhaps not even our own.[41] What we can and do see (and even come to know) is what Morris Rosenberg has called the "presenting self"—how we show ourselves to others, the image that we "manage" in our self-presentation.[42] For our purposes here, we have available for our study of the presenting self the composers' letters, journals, interviews, and autobiographical writings—in other words, their self-constructions. In addition, we have others' interpretations in the form of biographies and memoirs. We also have, of course, the artists' late creations, for they are the outcomes of their specifically artistic efforts, which function as what Rosenberg calls "ego-extensions."[43] These latter will be the constants in our study, since the range of other available materials is wide—from Verdi's frequent letters to his librettist as he was composing his last opera to Messiaen's rare and always carefully controlled—thus repetitive—interviews.

This external presentation of personhood is not all there is, needless to say. And it is also true that the external may be used to protect and conceal, rather than reveal, other internal, underlying aspects. Verdi memorably called this protective dimension his "armor of indifference."[44] What Carl Jung thought of as the "persona" and Simon Biggs as the "mask" are both related to this externalized part of personhood that negotiates with the social world.[45] That social world, in turn, comes to interpret and judge the person and his work differently over time, and that changing reception too is part of our interest in this book.

There is another important aspect to our stories of creative responses to the different challenges of aging: the fact that the presenting self of each composer is created, in part, through his articulating of a coherent and continuous narrative of himself as person and artist.[46] What Verdi, Strauss, Messiaen, and Britten all constructed—and reconstructed in the face of the challenges of aging—was an evolving narrative or life story that provided a sense of "unity, purpose and meaning."[47] To return to our opening image of the allegorical tapestry, these composers, like the frail stag, were indeed pursued by Old Age and her hounds, but they had a two-edged sword for defense: their artistic engagement may have precipitated, for each, a different later-life crisis, but it was also what offered the means to its successful resolution within that individual continuing life narrative.

CHAPTER TWO

Creative Responses to the Challenges of Aging

The eminent English novelist E. M. Forster (1879–1970), in his late years, adapted Herman Melville's novel *Billy Budd* for the operatic stage. In his libretto, he allowed one of the central characters, Captain Vere, to live on beyond the original plot and, as an old man, contemplate the life and death of one young man (the titular Billy). In this way, he framed the story and kept the focus on age and its search for enlightenment in the past. The seventy-year-old Forster had been depressed when he began this work, afraid he was losing the power to write, to feel, or even to take interest in people; Britten's invitation to write the libretto in 1949 began a process that, by the end, had revivified him personally and artistically.[1] As Nicholas Delbanco asserts in *Lastingness* (2011), the "habit of creation" need not die; indeed, it can be renewed.[2]

THE FOUR COMPOSERS AND THEIR PARTICULAR CHALLENGES

As a way of mapping the trajectory of this book and thus introducing both the figures who will form its core and their very personal responses to the challenges they faced with age, we turn to the late life and last works of someone who might appear to be an unlikely candidate for inclusion in a study of canonical composers: Jacques Offenbach (1818–1880). A famous German-born composer of French operetta, Offenbach led a complicated life, but his story foregrounds many of the different challenges faced by aging artists. For that reason, then, his turns out to be an uncannily appropriate tale for introducing and illuminating the lives of Verdi, Strauss, Messiaen, and Britten.

Toward the end of his life Offenbach struggled to create what was, in his eyes, his first and last serious opera, an "opéra fantastique" called *Les contes d'Hoffmann* (to a libretto by Jules Barbier, after the play by Barbier and Michel Carré). The famous composer of French operetta did not live to see the premiere of the work on which he labored longer than any other. Invested with his desire to create an artwork worthy of his talent, this was the opera that was to help him attain artistic legitimacy, the one that he hoped would make the world take him seriously as a composer not of operetta, but of opera. This major change in his creative activity—from the quick and easy composing of light and satiric comedies to a prolonged struggle and constant revising of a dramatic opera—mirrors, though in reverse, the change manifested in the late years of Italy's most famous composer of tragic opera, Giuseppe Verdi.

With his final work, *Falstaff* (1893), Verdi switched from tragedy to comedy, and did so with the same deliberation and, as it turned out, the same effort as Offenbach. Their motivations for these major changes, however, differed: the aging Offenbach sought to ensure a lasting and serious artistic legacy, while the even older Verdi, who already had a serious artistic legacy, wanted to influence the future of Italian opera. With his very different final work Verdi sought to teach a nationalistic lesson to young Italian composers, who he feared were being lured by the non-Italian seductions of the German operatic innovator Richard Wagner. The comic *Falstaff*'s sprightly and parodically echoing music was received by its audiences with surprise and puzzlement, yet also with a certain amount of nationalistic pride as creating a new direction for Italian opera. *Les contes d'Hoffmann* was just as much a surprise for those critics who saw Offenbach as a mere entertainer. Over the years it would be seen as "proof that with more creative time he might have become one of the foremost French composers of serious dramatic opera."[3] It would be accepted as Offenbach's "testament for posterity. Before such creative power . . . even his more prejudiced critics must fall silent."[4]

Why the prejudice of the critics? Some saw his operettas as "vulgar, lacking in style or passion, and often a satirical exploitation that was manipulated to exact humor at the cost of propriety, reverence, and taste."[5] No one contested his genius as a composer of such light works; what they would not allow him to do is move out of his assigned role of *l'amuseur*. For the French composer Camille Saint-Saëns, Offenbach "lost all his talent when he took himself seriously."[6] Offenbach himself complained to a friend that if he dared set foot in the Opéra or the Opéra-Comique, it was deemed a "sacrilege."[7] His early attempts to do so—the ballet *Papillon* at the Opéra and the opera *Barkouf* at the Opéra-Comique—had met with critical failure. His operettas, on the other hand, were the talk of Paris, not to mention Vienna, London, and New York. Rossini called Offenbach "the Mozart of the Champs-Elysées."[8]

The German child prodigy who came to Paris from Cologne as a youngster had begun composing these famous satirical French operettas in the 1840s and had reached the apogee of his success by the late 1860s, with audiences filling theaters on both sides of the Atlantic. In just over two years the prolific composer had three major successes: *La Grande-Duchesse de Gérolstein*, *La vie parisienne*, and *La belle Hélène*. Now a fully naturalized French citizen, he received the prestigious Légion d'honneur, and in 1867, during the Paris Exposition of that year, he himself was one of the main attractions: European royalty flocked to his operettas' many performances.[9]

All this changed with the outbreak of the short but disastrous Franco-Prussian War in 1870: in France Offenbach was considered a German, a *Prussien de coeur* (Prussian at heart);[10] in Germany he was seen as a traitor. In 1871, when he returned to Paris after spending the war outside France, he still faced opposition, either for having been too closely linked to the now defunct Second Empire or, on the other hand, for undermining it through his operettas' pointed satire. Either way, he had captured the mood and discovered the rhythm of the Second Empire,[11] but the mood of the Third Republic that succeeded it was very different, and Offenbach did not fare well in the Republican press. Puzzled at its vituperative invective and its lack of understanding of his satire *against* the Empire, the composer (who felt he was "French to the marrow of his bones")[12] was crushed when he was blamed for the frivolity and corruption of the regime—and thus for the French defeat. These attacks on his chosen nationality, combined with his personal financial distress and his nation's and especially his city's devastation in the Prussian occupation and the Paris Commune, created multiple threats to Offenbach's sense of himself—as a Frenchman, a Parisian, and a family provider, and also as a composer.

The political parallel here is to the last decades of the life of Richard Strauss, who would face even greater consequences for his fraught association with the National Socialist regime. Ever a German cultural nationalist, Strauss had, for a few brief years, accepted a position as the president of the Reichsmusikkammer, which controlled musical life under Hitler; fired because of his support of his Jewish librettist, Stefan Zweig, the composer spent World War II naively and ineptly attempting to deal with his disfavor with the Nazis and his worries about his Jewish daughter-in-law and grandsons. In those same years, Strauss, now in his early eighties, watched with great sorrow the destruction of his beloved German musical culture and the loss of all his meaningful social roles. With the theaters first closed and then destroyed by bombs, he felt the world as he knew it had come to an end. The postwar years brought multiple attacks on him for not leaving Nazi Germany. They also brought the tensions of denazification hearings and financial distress, as his assets were frozen by the victorious Allies. As with Offenbach, political and social upheaval brought severe challenges to personhood in his last years—challenges that Strauss met by conducting a musical "life review" of his work, an artistic stocktaking of his contribution to German musical culture.

The musical world changed radically after the war, sidelining Strauss in a newly avant-garde world. Likewise, Offenbach before him found that with the end of the Second Empire, the Parisian taste in operetta had quickly changed: Charles Lecocq was the new star in Paris, Johann Strauss Jr. in Vienna. Offenbach's frantic attempts to mount his works as grand spectacles met with both great success (*Orfée aux enfers*) and total disaster (*La haine*).[13] The now bankrupt (but still famous) composer then embarked on an American tour in the centenary year of 1876 to recoup his finances. Treated in the United States as a star, he enjoyed "the illusion of being the musical pacemaker of the glittering Second Empire."[14] Back in Paris he continued to compose new operettas that were not well received: he had not changed, but the times had.[15] What is telling is that he wrote these lighter pieces with speed and ease. In contrast, at the same time, he spent the next three years laboriously writing what he wanted to see as his masterpiece, *Les contes d'Hoffmann*. He clearly did not consider the operettas to be his artistic legacy—or, more accurately, perhaps he saw a successful and enduring "serious" dramatic opera as the work by which his talents deserved to be remembered.

Olivier Messiaen too chose to compose an opera in his later years—his only opera, *Saint François d'Assise*—that he intended as the summation of his career. The devoutly Catholic Messiaen was not a writer of light comic works; on the contrary, he was well-known as a composer of idiosyncratically avant-garde music with controversially religious import. The commission to compose an opera for the Paris Opéra challenged him not only to do something new but, in the process, to attempt to revolutionize the genre of opera—which he had deemed defunct. Moving, like Offenbach, out of the comfort zone of his usual compositional forms in his late years, Messiaen took much more time than expected to compose this operatic work that he thought of as his final legacy—musically, but also, in his case, religiously. And the cost of this high ambition to his physical and psychological well-being was extreme. Despite ill health and worries that he would not see the monumental work to its end, Messiaen, unlike Offenbach, did live to see performed the work he had consciously set up as his "opus ultimum." And thus, unlike Offenbach, he had to face the difficult question of what to do next—as both an artist and a religious man, that is, as a person.

Offenbach's health had been declining for many years: gout, arthritis, and rheumatism limited his mobility and caused great pain. But in his final years, this already very thin man began even more visibly to waste away, and, in his own eyes, he began to age: "The ravages of illness had aged him beyond his actual years and he was faced with the fact that he was *old*."[16] His sense of identity was threatened by both the physical pain and the double realization of aging and mortality. Benjamin Britten too, at the same age—his late fifties—had to face a premature "aging": because of a stroke suffered during cardiac surgery, the British concert pianist and composer was left impaired on his right side. This was in addition to the fact that the surgery did not relieve the symptoms, and thus the increasing physical limitations, caused by heart failure. Britten was suddenly, in his own view, catapulted into "old old age" and dependency. The comparison between the two composers does not end there. Both men had always been "working" composers, making their living from their compositions, and both saw themselves as productive and even driven workers. Their declining health with age and impairment made for challenges to this particular sense of their personhood, but both continued to create nonetheless. What the Viennese critic Eduard Hanslick said of Offenbach at the end of his life could have also been said of Britten: "To astounding facility of production, Offenbach united the most exemplary industry. . . . [Given] his self-command and patience, . . . ill and racked with pain, he would go on indefatigably working."[17] But fatigue and illness took their toll in the end.

As Offenbach feverishly composed his last work, his teenaged (and only) son was also ill with tuberculosis, tragically adding equally to the composer's sense of mortality and his thoughts of his legacy. He was famously described at this time as a "transparent, pale, sadly smiling ghost."[18] Part of what has been called the "biographical romance" surrounding the composition of *Les contes d'Hoffmann* projects Offenbach's own confrontation with aging, illness, and creativity onto the opera's story about the writer and composer E. T. A. Hoffmann.[19] Like the protagonist, who never attains any of his three loves in the opera, the composer, argued Siegfried Kracauer, felt he had "never attained the object of his love, grand opera. Like Hoffmann, he had been fooled by an evil spirit, who had estranged him from his true vocation. It seemed to him that he had blindly pursued false glory, and that he had wasted his precious gifts."[20] Identifying with other characters in the opera as well, the very ill Offenbach said he felt like the opera's mechanical doll, Olympia, who could collapse at any moment, or like Antonia, who would die were she to sing.[21] Yet despite his failing health, he persisted in composing, however slowly, desperate to finish the work in which he had placed all his hopes for his lasting artistic legacy.

It may seem a truism that age also brings with it increased thoughts of mortality, but as the gerontologist Victor W. Marshall has argued, there is actually an entirely new reality for the individual aging into old age to make sense of: the "self-as-mortal" or even "the self-as-dying."[22] This awareness is not a simple function of age but includes things like one's own health and the comparison of one's own age with the age at death of significant others in one's life. Like all the artists we studied, Offenbach too had to deal with the deaths of close friends and colleagues as he himself faced his own illness and mortality.

Britten's last opera, *Death in Venice*, composed in a race against time and surgery, can also, like Offenbach's final work, be read autobiographically as a tale of creativity and aging, as well as a story of homoerotic desire. The composer made a pact with his doctor: he would see a cardiologist if the physician would keep him going, with pharmaceutical assistance, until he finished the opera he knew would be his last. In a like vein, Offenbach wrote to a friend: "I have made a pact with Death. . . . I have said, 'If you let me finish my work in peace I shall be ready to follow you.'"[23] Offenbach died with everything but the orchestration of his opera completed. Britten underwent surgery after completing *Death in Venice* (1973), too ill to conduct the premiere, as was his wont. But he passionately wished his last opera to be the best thing he had ever written.[24] Clearly, with age and impending mortality, artistic extensions of personhood become charged with issues of worth—of both the self and the art. How those charged works are received by others, both at the time and later, can be quite another matter.

When Offenbach died in October 1880—in other words, before the premiere of *Les contes d'Hoffmann* in February 1881—the general response of the critics to the *amuseur* was clear. One frequent assessment can be summed up by a backhanded compliment in a British obituary: "Neither a musician nor a poet, but a master of catching, exciting, and rhythmical tune[,] . . . a man of his time."[25] With the premiere of *Les contes*, that denigrating assessment of Offenbach as simply an entertainer shifted somewhat. In time it would be said that in that last opera, "there was . . . a finesse, a touch of passion, an emotional depth which lifted this work to a height of artistry he had never previously attained."[26] But not all the critics were willing to change their minds. In 1919, the centenary of Offenbach's birth, one of them insisted that "his peculiar talent was scarcely fitted to work of a certain depth," as proved by the failure of his earlier attempts at opera—a failure "but partially redeemed by the *Tales of Hoffmann*."[27]

LAST WORKS AND "LATE STYLE"

It is not at all rare to see—either at the time or afterward—simultaneous positive and negative assessments of the last works and what is called the "late style" of an aging artist. The reception of Offenbach's opera is obviously no exception, though more complicated than most because of the posthumous premiere of *Les contes d'Hoffmann*. Before that work opened, the critics declared at his death that "his later works showed every sign that his genius was on the wane. Indeed, when we reflect that M. Offenbach had reached the age of sixty-one, we cannot be surprised that his powers of creation were not as fresh as of yore."[28] The same obituary lamented that he had not turned his attention to "the higher branches of his art, for which not a few of his works seem, in the midst of their frivolity, to hint at undeveloped capacities." Of course, he had so turned his attention, but the work that would prove it had not yet been premiered. In Vienna, Hanslick wrote that "musical talent of a perfectly unusual order and a brilliant specialty have passed away with Offenbach."[29] But even he went on to claim that the composer "grew weary in the concluding years, and though still wonderfully fertile, gave us as a rule only a weak reflex of his former compositions." A familiar narrative of decline with age and illness dominated the obituaries. In only a few months, of course, what were considered both the last work and its composer's late style would change radically. A new assessment was in order. For some, as we have seen, the opera didn't change much, only "partially" redeeming his career; but there were others who would come to see the opera as his lasting legacy and its late style as proof that he was "a genius capable of composing weighty music with profound passion."[30]

As Anthony Barone has explored in great detail in his study of Richard Wagner's last work, there is a long history, across art forms and historical periods, of such simultaneous and contradictory assessments of late style.[31] These begin in the ancient world and develop through the Renaissance to their more canonical articulations in the German romantic era.

By the nineteenth century, as Barone demonstrates, two opposing models of creativity in late age had come into being. One was the familiar, biologically inspired one of maturation to a peak followed by decline and degeneration that haunted Offenbach's obituaries. In contrast, there was Goethe's aesthetic and metaphysical narrative of apotheosis and transcendence in the last years of an artist's life: with age come contemplation, greater life experience, more spiritual insight, greater understanding—all leading not only to technical advancement but, implied Goethe, to epiphany, a withdrawal from outward appearances, and an emphasis on essentials.[32] As a result, by the time of Offenbach's death an aesthetic and spiritual redemptivist discourse of late style vied with one of biological and creative degeneration in which the dynamism of youth yielded to the inevitable obsolescence of age. And Offenbach, like all of the composers we study here, was aware of both the existence and the power of this cultural discourse around creativity, aging, and late works. To some extent, each of these artists fashioned not only his last works but also his evolving life narrative in such a way as to try to control the final evaluation of his career and legacy.

While many artists' lives, like Offenbach's, may easily be interpreted using one or the other of these generalized models, what has become more evident to us is the unique nature of artists' later years and late styles, in the plural.[33] To generalize about older composers is not our aim, in other words, though this is a common tendency—across disciplines—in writing about age. The notion that all older people are pretty much the same has been identified as one of the six major myths about the elderly.[34] We believe that comparable generalizations about artists' late works have the potential to be equally ageist. Each artist we study began his career in an individual manner; he also ended it in an individual way. What we investigate is the complexity of the interrelationship between aging and creativity in all its individuality and contingency; we avoid having recourse to the more common transhistorical, transcultural, supraindividual universalizing that has characterized late-style discourse for centuries, from Giorgio Vasari in the Renaissance through to Edward Said in our own time. There is arguably such a thing as an artist's *individual* "late style," but it develops as the result of an entire lifetime of creations and personal history. Once an artist dies, this term (as defined and used by critics) becomes "invested in works as part of their reception, and thus becomes part of their historical baggage."[35] What is at stake, as we have seen with Offenbach, is nothing less than the reputation and retrospective evaluation of an artist's entire oeuvre. Sometimes this designation of late style is a sentimentalizing act: we are intended to witness the great truths and insights imparted in the final works, read as the definitive final testaments. Sometimes it is a debunking move: we are shown how the artist "lost it" at the end, and thus why final works can simply be ignored or dismissed. Either way, the defining and valuing of an artist's particular late style is always a retrospective *critical* construct with its own aesthetic and ideological agenda and, most important, its own view of both aging and creativity.

And it is the aesthetic values of the *critic* that in the end really do determine what in particular is deemed positive or negative in the last works of an artist. Therefore, if you are a late-romantic Georg Simmel or an Albert Erich Brinckmann, you appreciate wholeness, coherence, synthesis; older age becomes a time of reappraisal, summary, consolidation. But if you're a modernist (and Marxist-inflected) Adorno or a Said, you treasure fragmentation, dissonance, lack (or impossibility) of reconciliation.[36] In Gordon McMullan's cogent terms, any universalizing discourse of lateness is "a construct, ideological, rhetorical and heuristic, a function not of life or of art but of the practice of reading or appreciating certain texts within a set of predetermined parameters."[37]

In exploring the last works and late lives of Verdi, Strauss, Messiaen, and Britten, we discovered that there were more differences than similarities both in composers' personalities and in their life circumstances. Some of these lived in times of social and political unrest that either hindered or spurred their creativity. Some had personal lives that impeded or, sometimes, promoted their work. Some were healthy, some faced disability. Nevertheless, while their late styles are resolutely individual and unique, as suggested in this chapter, there are indeed shared challenges that arise from the relationship between age and creativity as it has played out in the last two centuries in the West. Among these are aesthetic age-related issues: worries of being "left behind," of being supplanted by a younger generation. Other shared challenges are cultural and even national, since each was considered a foremost composer in his time and place. Each, because he was both older and famous, had high expectations of himself. In addition, and even more stressfully, each knew his last works would be judged by others differently and more critically from the preceding ones. The responses to this realization, however, were deeply individual. As we shall see in the next chapter, Verdi consistently downplayed the importance of his last works, claiming he was only composing for his own enjoyment, when in fact he was on a pedagogical mission to rescue Italian opera. Messiaen decided to use his only foray into the genre of opera to change the form itself—and ended up biting off almost more than he could chew.

CHANGE AND MODERNISM

The years that separated the late works of Verdi from those of Messiaen were also the ones that saw the rise of musical modernism, first in Paris and Vienna, before spreading throughout the Western world. The potent combination of the emphasis on aesthetic progress and innovation within musical modernism and the drive toward change and renewal within the entire culture of modernity constituted a force, as we shall see, with which these older composers had to contend.

Offenbach chose artistic change in his last years; so too did Verdi and Messiaen. Strauss and Britten arguably did not. To understand how this choice played out over time—and in the modern age—let us return to that discourse of late style and those two models of later life creativity that have continued to coexist in our own time: the organicist one of decline and the metaphysical one of transcendence with age. Each of these has in turn come to be discussed in terms of two opposing forms of late style—rupture and continuity.[38] Thus, depending on the model adopted, each form can have either a positive or a negative evaluation at the time of reception and later. That is, a final work can be seen as marking a rupture (in either style or content) in an artist's oeuvre, as was the case with the great operatic tragedian, Verdi, premiering his only comedy,[39] *Falstaff*, when he was almost eighty years old. Viewed according to the transcendence model, this break from his past practice was interpreted as a sign of liberating personal renewal, one that might in fact make the work itself stand outside his own time and thus point the way to the future of the entire art form. But seen from the perspective of the decline model, the comedy could also be cited as proof that the artist was clearly past his prime and was no longer capable of writing those great tragedies.[40]

On the other hand, when there is no rupture, that is, when a late work continues on in the manner of all the others that came before it, that can be interpreted either as the height of technical or spiritual mastery—and thus the summation of a career and proof of a constant aesthetic—or as a sign that the aging artist is incapable of innovation at this late stage of life. Richard Strauss's metamusical, recapitulative late works (at least those preceding the *Four Last Songs* [*Vier letzte Lieder*]) have certainly been read in both ways.[41] In other words, the late artist is seen either as being in the fullness of his powers or else as becoming set in his ways and simply repeating himself.[42]

With the advent of musical modernism in the 1890s, however, the particular form of rupture or change in late works in particular took on even more positive aesthetic weight. In Daniel Albright's words, musical modernism became "a testing of the limits of aesthetic construction" and involved "a strong thrust towards the verges of the aesthetic experience."[43] In this new ideological and artistic framework, revivifying experimentation and pushing formal limits came to be fundamental. The prevailing values of cultural modernity, in general, further reinforced this aesthetic valuing of change and progress. In this sense, we might see Verdi's change to a new and very different style of composition at the end of his career as progressive (though certainly not musically modernist).

With modernism, all aspects of the music of the common-practice era (that is, from the baroque period to the end of romanticism) were now open to innovation. Following Wagner, Strauss and Gustav Mahler expanded temporal duration and sonic resources to "maximalize" expression in both symphony and opera.[44] Experiments with whole-tone scales by Claude Debussy, with octatonic scales by Nicolai Rimsky-Korsakov, Alexander Scriabin, and Igor Stravinsky, and with the "pantonality" of Arnold Schoenberg challenged the functional relationships of traditional musical language. These "extensions and destruction of tonality"[45]—made possible by Wagner's harmonic innovations—created a new harmonic idiom with which every composer thereafter would have to deal. The modernist search for change and revivification went further and in other directions as well, ranging from an exploration of the intervals and melodies of folk music by Béla Bartók and Leoš Janáček to the reconsideration of preromantic forms in the neoclassicism of Stravinsky. These aspects of musical modernism evolved not as one but, rather, as a "spectrum of styles . . . and the styles themselves so mutually hostile."[46] What united them conceptually was that ethos of change, innovation, originality, and progress against which both composers and their compositions were judged: in this sense, modernism "locat[ed] the value of the composition not inside the composition itself, but inside the meta-narrative: a story about aesthetic progressivity."[47] Composers who did not meet the standards of progress demanded by this ideology were dismissed as either old-fashioned or irrelevant. Given the dissonance and chromaticism of his early works *Salome* (1905) and *Elektra* (1909) Richard Strauss was initially seen as a part of the modernist avant-garde. When he reverted to, and continued writing in, a more traditional style of composition, he was dismissed by modernist critics, for whom this move marked the beginning of his long, slow, and inexorable decline.

After World War II modernism, particularly in the form of serial music, made a comeback, supported by institutions such as the Darmstadt

International Summer Courses for New Music and the Donaueschingen
Festival of Contemporary Music. Serial music took on a politically positive resonance, in part because it had been banned as degenerate (*entartet*)
by the National Socialists, and consequently it was now happily dissoci-
ated from that compromised Nazi past.[48] Because of the times in which
Messiaen and Britten lived, throughout their entire compositional careers
they had to deal with the musical changes of modernism as a constant
pressure, and each had different ways of doing so. Messiaen was exposed to
serialism, especially as practiced by Anton Webern, through his students
Pierre Boulez and Karlheinz Stockhausen, and through his own participation in the Darmstadt summer school. After a period of experimentation with this compositional process, Messiaen turned to his own idiosyncratic, innovative rhythmic and harmonic techniques. These offered
him a late-modernist musical idiom that not only was totally different but
also was employed to new, specifically religious ends.[49] Britten's primarily
tonal but very eclectic and distinctive musical language was influenced by
a wide range of sources—from Balinese gamelan to serialism to his friendship with Dmitri Shostakovich. Neither twentieth-century composer was
viewed as central to the modernist program, but, like Strauss and Verdi,
both were inevitably judged in their time by its aesthetic criteria. This
is because for a time in that century the conservatories and the academy
became bastions of modernist ideology, judging musical works according
to their particular aesthetic and ideological program. In our current, more
pluralist and eclectic musical milieu, the practices of modernism form
only part of the tool kit of contemporary composers, and today's critics are
in the process of reevaluating the works and creators of modernism as well
as of those once devalued by the modernist dominance.

⸰◌⸰

Offenbach's rich story of resilience, defiance, and creativity in confront-
ing the many and diverse challenges of aging has allowed us to introduce
Verdi, Strauss, Messiaen, and Britten, along with the particular challenges
they faced—ranging from generational anxieties to ill health and impairment. But later life offers opportunities along with the inevitable challenges. These composers' final works and their self-fashioning of their presenting selves testify to their unique responses to both.

CHAPTER THREE

Giuseppe Verdi (1813–1901):
A Generational Tale of Cultural Nationalism

I should have been able to stand, so to speak, with one foot in the past, and the other in the present and future (for I have no fear of the "music of the future").
—Giuseppe Verdi, letter to Francesco Florimo

In 1863 in Milan, a rebellious twenty-one-year-old poet and composer wrote an ode excoriating what he considered to be the provincial and old-fashioned art of his country. He declaimed his poem at a banquet on the occasion of the premiere of the first opera of his good friend Franco Faccio. The ode included a rather strong image intended as praise for his young friend: "Perhaps the man is already born who, modest and pure, will restore art to its altar—now stained like a brothel wall."[1]

Giuseppe Verdi, the acclaimed composer of two dozen operas up to this point—among them *Rigoletto* (1851), *La traviata* (1853), and *La forza del destino* (1862)—could not help feeling he was being targeted by this line, and was duly offended by this image of Italian art as besmirched.[2] And so begins this long tale of generational differences. The historical irony is that the radical young poet who penned that ode was none other than Arrigo Boito, the man who, more than twenty years later, would become the seventy-four-year-old Verdi's last (and, some would say, best) librettist. In 1863, however, the fifty-year-old composer was not wrong to feel personally insulted.

The young Boito and Faccio were part of a generation that felt strongly that Italian music was in dire need of revitalization and that the dominance of opera had led to the atrophy of an Italian instrumental tradition, leaving their country behind, lagging in the wake of the German symphonic innovations sweeping Europe. The recently unified nation called

Italy, they felt, had to move beyond the political and cultural ideals of the Risorgimento, the social and political movement that had brought about the first iteration of the new Italian state. And in music, this meant moving beyond Verdi and the Italian operatic tradition of the day. These two young men, then in their early twenties, were members of a Milanese movement of bohemian artists, writers, and composers known as the Scapigliatura. The *scapigliati* (literally, "disheveled ones") were self-consciously nonconformist and passionately dedicated to reforming, that is, to internationalizing and modernizing what they saw as their parochial and conventional Italian culture—mainly by opening it up to what was happening in France and, in particular, Germany.[3]

On a celebratory trip to Paris following their graduation from the Milan Conservatory, Faccio and Boito met the poet Charles Baudelaire, as infamous for his bohemian lifestyle as for his 1857 volume of poems, *Les fleurs du mal*. With his recent publication of *Richard Wagner et Tannhauser* [sic] *à Paris*, French Wagnerism had been born. Popular among individuals who "shared deep reservations about aspects of their society and culture and were looking for a vital new alternative,"[4] Wagnerism, as it played out over time, was never a completely coherent notion, and what is interesting is that it was initially based not on Wagner's music but rather on his revolutionary theoretical writings, published from 1848 to 1851 while the composer was in exile in Switzerland.[5] Baudelaire, however, had attended both the 1861 Paris premiere of *Tannhäuser* and the three concerts Wagner had conducted leading up to it. At the latter, he wrote to Wagner, he had experienced the greatest musical rapture ("la plus grande juissance musicale") of his life.[6]

In Paris Boito and Faccio also met Giuseppe Verdi, Wagner's exact contemporary (both had been born in 1813). Now, at the age of forty-eight, both composers were eager for a major success in Paris—long accepted as "opera central" in Europe and at the time ruled by the *grand opéra* of Giacomo Meyerbeer.[7] In 1861, however, Verdi and Wagner were at different stages of their careers: Wagner's most significant operas were yet to come, but Verdi was already established as the most important Italian opera composer of his time. Yet it was Wagner, with his concept of the "artwork of the future," who was being promoted in Europe as the new radical voice by the New German School centered in Weimar on Franz Liszt and the contentious journal *Neue Zeitschrift für Musik*. Verdi, on the other hand, was firmly associated not with the future, necessarily, but certainly with Italy's present and past: politically, elected as deputy to the new parliament of the united Italy in Turin, as well as culturally, seen as (or constructed as) the patriotic hero, the cultural icon of the Risorgimento. In part because of Verdi, opera was seen as the best cultural medium to create a much needed sense of shared Italian identity—*italianità*.[8]

GENERATIONAL DYNAMICS: GERMAN VERSUS ITALIAN MUSIC

The younger generation of Italians was not so pleased with what it saw as an exhausted culture in serious need of renewal. Wagner was one of those to whom they looked for that revitalization. Even though Boito worked happily with Verdi, writing the lyrics for his *Inno delle nazioni* in 1862, it was Wagner, the revolutionary theorist, whom he saw as leading the way forward. Hence his implied insult to Verdi in his 1863 ode, and Verdi's personal and nationalistic resentment of it.

The German Wagner and the Italian Verdi were opposites in just about every way imaginable, from the temperamental to the cultural, as Peter Conrad has explored in detail.[9] Likely destined by their shared birth year to be rivals, they never met in person, to anyone's knowledge, and had very different attitudes toward one another. Wagner's few recorded comments about Verdi are mostly mocking and dismissive; Verdi, on the other hand, was forced to pay attention to Wagner and even take him seriously, in part because of the attraction of the younger generation of Italian opera composers to his ideas.

Given that Verdi and his predecessors had made the *voice* and *melody* the touchstones of Italian opera, what Wagner was offering was an utterly un-Italian, that is, German, instrumental emphasis on the *orchestra* and *harmony*. Wagner was also a theorist, writing at length about his ideas; Verdi scorned theory, arguing for the spontaneous and the instinctive that he saw as particularly Italian. Verdi articulated the profound differences between the two nations' concepts of music:

> Since the Germans have other artistic methods than we have, their art is basically different from ours. We cannot compose like the Germans, or at least we ought not to; nor they like us. Let the Germans assimilate our artistic substance, as Haydn and Mozart did in their time; yet they remained predominantly symphonic musicians. . . . But if we let fashion, love of innovation, and an alleged scientific spirit tempt us to surrender the native quality of our own art, the free natural certainty of our work and perception, our bright golden light, then we are simply being stupid and senseless.[10]

Verdi would repeat the need to retain this crucial difference between Germans and Italians in his letters throughout his life; he never gave up his feeling that the innovations of his German rival and competitor were a serious threat to the Italian operatic tradition to which he was still contributing so much. (That this history has resonance even today was made clear by the consternation of Italians when La Scala chose to open the Verdi/Wagner 2013 bicentenary season not with Verdi but with—Wagner.)[11]

In Paris in 1866 Verdi heard the overture to *Tannhäuser*, and his first reaction was to declare that Wagner was "mad."[12] He was aware of the closing of *Tannhäuser* in Paris after only three performances and asked for details—*and* for copies of Wagner's complete prose works and the opera's score.[13] In November 1871 the Teatro Communale in Bologna presented the first Wagner opera ever to be performed in Italy: *Lohengrin*. Boito was ecstatic, writing to Wagner himself about his enthusiastic reaction—to which Wagner responded with "A Letter to a Young Italian Friend." Verdi was curious. With the *Lohengrin* score in hand, he secretly made his way to Bologna by train, incognito, so to speak—only to be recognized on the platform by the opera's conductor. "Outed" publicly at the theater that night, he refused to acknowledge the crowd's cries of "Viva Verdi!"

Personal competition and cultural nationalism likely merged in Verdi's suspicion of Wagner's influence, that is, of his seduction of the younger Italian generation. As time passed, that influence grew even stronger, as Wagner's works began to be performed in Italy. To his intense irritation, Verdi himself would soon be accused of coming under that influence and imitating Wagner.[14] The German's radical harmonic language, especially the chromaticism of *Tristan und Isolde* (1865) and the dissonances of *Parsifal* (1882), pushed conventional tonality toward the breaking point that would become musical modernism. As James Hepokoski put it, "[In] an increasingly Wagnerian, symphonic, and intellectually skeptical age, Verdi surely believed that he was upholding the primacy of the voice, the dominance of diatonic melody, the direct outpouring of elemental, instantly communicable emotions, and the attracting of as large a public as possible."[15] But for the rest of his life Verdi continued to worry about the impact of this creeping "Germanism" on Italian music. His life circumstances were also changing in these years. Financially comfortable by this point, Verdi often wrote in his letters about retiring from opera composing altogether, and after *Aida* in 1871, at the age of fifty-eight, that is effectively what he did. He bought a working farm, Sant'Agata, near his native Busseto and wrote no new operas for the next sixteen years.

In 1883, when Richard Wagner died, Verdi wrote to his publisher, Giulio Ricordi: "A great individualist [has] disappeared! A name that leaves a very powerful mark on the history of Art."[16] It was the very power of that mark that had in fact always worried Verdi. As we have seen, what he saw as the German's intellectual, systematic theorization was anathema to him, the contrary of his concept of the Italian lyric imagination and its emotional power over the hearts of audiences—and young composers. He wrote to a friend: "Art and systems are opposed to each other, and those who adhere to a systematic preconceived idea are wrong for they sacrifice their imagination and their gifts. For that reason, the influence of the colossal, very great Wagner was harmful."[17] Despite his admiration for his rival, only weeks before Wagner's death Verdi had written:

> Nowadays there are no students or teachers who have not been infected with Germanism, and it would hardly be possible to pick a commission free of this sickness; the disease, like any other, must run its course.
>
> Our music differs from German music. Their symphonies can live in halls; their chamber music can live in the home. Our music, I say, resides principally in the theater.[18]

And to the theater Verdi would return.

LATE STYLE

There is little evidence to support novelist Franz Werfel's thesis (in his 1925 fictional *Verdi: A Novel of the Opera*) that it was Wagner's death that liberated an exhausted and depressed elderly Verdi to fight on for the hearts and souls of the younger generation of Italian composers. What in fact brought Verdi back to composing for the theater was an elaborate plot instigated by his publisher, Ricordi, and his friend (and now favorite conductor) Faccio—the very dedicatee of Boito's ode. And their plot ensured that it would be Boito who would be the librettist of Verdi's final tragic masterpiece, *Otello*—which premiered in 1887 when the composer was seventy-four years old.

Everyone, including Verdi, assumed this would be his last opera. While he was composing *Otello*, the composer wrote to his librettist: "Too much time has gone by! The years of my age are too many! And too many my YEARS OF SERVICE!!!! I wouldn't want the public to have to say to me too obviously, '*Enough!*'"[19] The reviewers said no such thing, of course, but they did assume this was to be his final opera. Blanche Roosevelt, an

American singer and writer, announced that the artist was "more Verdi than ever" and labeled the opera "the last work of a great man."[20] Had this indeed been Verdi's last opera, then everyone would have seen *Otello* as the crowning achievement of a master of tragic opera. For example, Camille Bellaigue wrote in the *Revue des deux mondes*: "Never has a more constant glory shed its rays for a longer time upon a human brow. He has known neither shadow nor decline, and his star will go out as upon those blessed horizons that do not know the sadness of twilight and retain until the final hour all the splendor of their sun."[21]

To see the last work, as so many did in this case, as an apotheosis, as the culmination of a career, as an aesthetic and philosophical synthesis, is to see older age as the time of reappraisal and the older artist as master of his craft. As we noted in the last chapter, thanks to the musings upon age and creativity of the long-lived German writer Goethe, there existed in Europe at this time a positive model for the aging artist. By the time of *Otello*'s premiere, this was certainly the reigning discourse in Europe about Verdi. Had he stopped composing at this point, this would certainly have been the view that dominated.

Interestingly, when *Otello* premiered, it was also seen as decidedly Wagnerian— that is, more through-composed, more harmonically complex than anything Verdi had composed before. We know that Verdi asked Ricordi for scores of *Die Meistersinger* and *Parsifal* when he was writing the opera.[22] After the premiere, Antonio Fogazzaro went so far as to claim: "*Otello* marks a new evolution in Verdi's style, a step to what is called music of the future."[23] Verdi disagreed, of course. Nevertheless, by this time a tendency toward through-composition and a more symphonic approach had become the new norm in Italian opera too.[24] *Otello* was nonetheless received as the summa of Verdi's long career as a composer of Italian tragic opera. His advanced years were inevitably a marked feature of that reception.

In Verdi's own eyes, it was time to return to being a gentleman farmer at Sant'Agata. He was in excellent health for his age; indeed, the hypochondria and minor afflictions of his earlier years seemed to have disappeared. Unlike the proudly hypersensitive and delicate Wagner, Verdi was proudly vigorous and robust. Despite his retirement, Verdi continued to worry about that creeping Germanism, writing in July 1889 to Faccio, who had just conducted the London premiere of *Otello*:

You speak of a "triumph of Italian art"!! You deceive yourself! Our young Italian composers are not good patriots. If the Germans, stemming from Bach, arrive at Wagner, they are doing as good Germans should, and that's fine. But for us, descendents of Palestrina, to imitate Wagner is to commit a musical crime, and we are doing something useless, even harmful.[25]

It was just about this time that the now seventy-eight-year-old Verdi received an enticement from Boito: "There is only one way to end better than with *Otello*, and this is to end victoriously with *Falstaff*. Having made all the cries and lamentations of the human heart resound, to end with an immense outburst of cheer! That will astonish!"[26]

Though in fine health, Verdi was getting older and feeling his age. Initially reluctant, he had pleaded "the enormous number of my years" to Boito and feared that the effort might be too much for him, and that if he were not to finish the music, his younger librettist would have wasted much time and effort.[27] Nevertheless, Verdi agreed: "Let us do *Falstaff* then! We will not think for the moment about the obstacles, age, illnesses!"[28] Over the next four years Verdi and Boito would continue their fruitful collaboration in secrecy (or attempted secrecy) both in person and on paper—writing detailed letters to each other regularly about everything from plot details to prosody, from theatrical effects to casting.[29] In the end, together they produced *Falstaff*, their adaptation for the operatic stage of Shakespeare's *The Merry Wives of Windsor*. This last work did indeed "astonish," not only because of Verdi's advanced years but, as Boito knew, because the great composer of tragic opera had turned to the genre of comedy for his final work.[30] And we would argue that he did so for a specific purpose, a pedagogical purpose: the opera was targeted specifically at the young Wagner-besotted Italian composers of his day. As Parker puts it, in *Falstaff* Verdi offered "a kind of manifesto, an ideological statement, an attempt to influence the story of Italian opera."[31] Boito knew exactly how to appeal to Verdi, writing to him during the composition: "In the name of Shakespeare, give Art and our country another, new victory."[32]

Boito masterfully adapted Shakespeare's play about the elderly knight's attempt to woo Alice Ford and Meg Page, the "merry wives of Windsor." It is a comic tale of jealousy (that of Alice's husband, Ford) and thwarted young love (between Alice's daughter, Nannetta, and Fenton). A story of generational conflict, the Italian operatic version also focuses on an aging man's continuing sensual pleasures—wine, women, and song, one could say—even though he is destined for a comeuppance for his boldness. We know that the libretto tempted Verdi because of its linguistic wit and comic verve, and because it offered him a chance to do something very different from his previous works. Going beyond Shakespeare's *Merry Wives* to include Falstaff's portrayal in *Henry IV, Parts 1* and *2*, Boito created a memorable, larger-than-life—and older—character for what Verdi called "a lyric comedy . . . unlike any other. . . . Falstaff is a rascal who commits all kinds of wickedness . . . but in a jolly way."[33] Boito went out of his way to convince Verdi that Shakespeare's source for the Falstaff character was indeed Italian,[34] so his story could be used in this didactic exercise in *italianità*. Verdi openly admitted that he was also attracted to Boito's "merry" libretto because it cheered him up and made him burst into laughter,[35] for it was in these years that he began to face many more of those human challenges of aging.

As he began composing, he had to deal with the deaths of two of his closest friends, as well as the tragic and ultimately fatal illness of Franco Faccio. Noting that these were all men who were younger than himself, Verdi wrote to a friend in December 1890: "Everything is ending! Life is a sad business! I leave you to imagine the sorrow I felt, and still feel! And that is why I am not very keen to continue writing an opera which I have begun, but not got very far with. Pay no attention to what you read in the newspapers. Will I finish it? Will I not finish it? Who knows? I am writing without a schedule, with no object in mind, other than to pass a few hours each day."[36] The claim that he was writing the opera only for his own amusement became a refrain in his letters over the next years—perhaps out of self-protection or to control (or at least lower) expectations, or perhaps to keep his persistent publisher at bay.

In a letter to Ricordi in which he insisted that he was merely writing *Falstaff* "to pass the time. . . . I repeat, *to pass the time!* Nothing else!," he went on to point out another of the challenges he was facing: "When I was young, even when ailing, I could stay at my desk for 10, even 12 hours, always working, without taking a breath. Then I had command of my body and time.—Today, alas, I do not."[37] Limited in his energy, Verdi worked more slowly than he ever had before. But write he did, for he had a cultural mission, one he articulated to the eminent German conductor Hans von Bülow: "You are fortunate to be still the sons of Bach. But we? We, the sons of Palestrina, once had a great school, and it was our own. Now it is a bastard growth and ruin threatens. Can we begin again?"[38] *Falstaff* was intended as that new beginning.

After many fits and starts, Verdi and Boito finally finished their comic opera; it was premiered at La Scala in Milan in February 1893. Within the next few years the opera would be staged around the world, but it was first received in Italy with both "inflated nationalistic rapture, as a sublime manifestation of *italianità*, and puzzlement at its novelty and lack of immediate appeal to the general public—those who had the misfortune to be uninitiated."[39] There *was* an initiate, however—the cohort of those young Italian composers. Cultural nationalism in the 1890s implicitly demanded of that next generation that they renovate the genre of Italian opera in order to restore Italy to its former musical supremacy. And Verdi was going to show them the way.

Nevertheless, when the opera was premiered, audiences and critics alike were baffled: *Falstaff* both sounded the same (for it echoed his earlier operas) and yet was different. The young lovers, Fenton and Nannetta, for example, have a beautiful love duet, very much like those of the middle-period operas, but each time they begin it, they are interrupted by the stage action. Where were what one review called "the broad melodies that had decorated the earlier operas"? Where were the usual finales?[40] Well, they simply weren't there. Instead, the audience heard fragmentation, bursts of melody, a great diversity of rhythms and orchestration. As one critic later put it, Verdi "scatters tunes about as though he were trying to give them away."[41] He also scattered echoes around—of his own works and those of many others, as we shall see.

From his letters we know that Verdi was consciously trying to do something different from what he had done before and also from the Italian opera buffa tradition. It was to be something new but still Italian—something he called a *commedia lirica*.[42] The music, he told Ricordi, would have to be sung differently than that of other comic operas,[43] for he was writing a comedy "in which the rapid flow of the dialogue and the play of facial expressions are the principal features."[44] After his wife went to a rehearsal for the first time, she wrote to her sister: "On first impression, it appears to be a new genre, even the beginning of a whole new art of music and poetry!"[45] The music was certainly different in many ways from what everyone was expecting, leading critics to use such terms as "lavishness of invention" and "melodic prodigality."[46] Some have viewed its musical diversity as the result of Verdi's sensitivity to the words of Boito's lively libretto; others sensed he was playing on his audience's expectations, offering them something that both sounded familiar and yet was disconcertingly different. Indeed, Hepokoski would later find *Falstaff* "both formally progressive and profoundly traditional."[47] It was that echoing quality, we would argue, that accounted for this paradox.

Not surprisingly, when the many echoes of his own previous operas, *Otello* in particular, were noticed in the new work, that other, more negative view of creative lateness was invoked: lateness as exhaustion and ob solescence. As we saw in the last chapter, this discourse of late creativity, drawn equally from biological theories of age and decline and romantic idealization of youthful energy, saw the last works of an artist as manifesting the effects of age and the imminence of death. According to this model, the works of an artist's late style can only be seen negatively: continuity of style is considered repetition, lacking the spark of youthful genius. (Indeed, Bruno Barilli described *Falstaff* as "cooling lava without fire.")[48] But if an artist changed his style in his last years, as Verdi obviously did here, the rupture was seen as bizarre—too different, too new, too unexpected.

Not everyone felt that way about *Falstaff*, of course, neither then nor now. But curiously, even when they praised the work, they all pointed to Verdi's advanced age (he was seventy-nine), as well as to the work's differences—in genre and style—from all his earlier operas. For one reviewer, he was still "the glorious old man who lighted the spark of life."[49] Another wrote, "What an unexpectedly beautiful, significant turn to find the old man, toward the end of his life, breaking away from tragedy and, with the wisdom of blessed age, resting his gaze on the sunny, humorous side of existence!"[50] As we have also seen, there is also a positive reading of late creativity that sees a stylistic rupture like Verdi's as reflecting a new energy, a liberating of the repressed, a renewal through experimentation, and a deconstructing of the artist's earlier work. If art produced by this kind of break is not easily understandable at the time of its creation, the argument goes, that is not surprising, for in a very real sense this late art is not "of its time": it is for future generations to appreciate the radical newness in this late style. We want to argue, however, that *Falstaff* and thus Verdi's late style in fact mark both continuity and rupture, a link to the past of Italian opera and a pointing toward its future for the next generation of young composers.[51]

SELF-PARODY

The reason this doubleness is possible is that the form Verdi uses is parody, a time-honored mode of marking (but with irony) both difference and similarity, of simultaneously incorporating (but distancing) the past and moving forward in new directions.[52] He could make the jealousy of the character Ford in *Falstaff* echo Otello in his jealous rage, but the irony and the new comic context would together mark the important difference of perspective, as we shall see shortly. Commentators on *Falstaff*'s music have often noted what they call its "echoing" quality, something that makes it sound "old and at the same time new."[53] As one puts it, "Verdi brought an era to an end by summing up all that was best in it."[54] And, since much of what was "best in it" was his own work, it is no surprise that he would echo himself, as well as others, in his last opera. But the switch from the tragic to the comic genre permitted Verdi's music to change. The echoing of his own earlier work functioned as a way for him to recontextualize— through the distancing power of irony—his own work within the larger context of the history of opera *and* from the perspective of age and experience. This was his way of suggesting the direction in which he thought Italian opera should move. Liberated from repetition by the shift to comedy, the composer could comment upon his grand tragic themes and their musical enactment—but with humor and wit, and not a little continuing sympathy—as a way of creating something new.

Verdi's comic self-parodies in *Falstaff* provided a new context for his own tragic melodic gestures and themes, creating in the ears of his audience both continuations of and departures from the Verdian past. His familiar thematic preoccupations were all there but rendered ironic in their new context: love opposed by a hostile father, jealousy, adultery, honor. The most often cited example of the musical and thematic shift from the tragic to the comic register, from the painful to the funny, is indeed Otello's fury in relation to Ford's jealousy. Ford's aria in *Falstaff*, act 2, part 1, is sometimes seen as a bit of tragedy inserted into a comedy, totally convincing in its pain and thus invoking our sympathy. Yet despite its musically convincing echo of Otello's dark rage and sorrow, the passage is in fact doubly inappropriate in its new context: not only is this a comedy (and that generic framing conditions our response to the scene), but we have already seen Alice Ford plotting against Falstaff—who is not any real threat to Ford, as he himself would know were he not so jealous. But the parodic suggestion of Otello's music has yet another function: jealousy in this case may be silly, but it is still potentially dangerous, as the plot of *Otello* makes clear. This adds a tension to the scene and an urgency to the women's plot. Following Ford's aria, Falstaff returns to the stage, introduced by a series of trills. These recall not only the trills of the knight's self-satisfied celebration of his own phallic power earlier (as we shall see) in the "Va, vecchio John" passage that precedes Ford's entry, but also the "writhing trills" of Jago's Credo.[55] The music that links the foolish Falstaff to the evil Jago suggests a further ironizing of the relationship between Ford and Otello.

Many other echoes of Verdi's last tragic opera have been noted, but the larger issue is: why would Verdi select this and other of his works (and typical manners) to be put to ironic use? By way of a possible response, we would like to consider how self-parody functions in the opera's final scene as the disguised merry wives torment Falstaff. To music that echoes the "Hostias" and the "Ingemisco" from Verdi's own *Messa da Requiem*, the women mockingly pray that God make Falstaff chaste: "Domine fallo casto!" Falstaff replies with an almost sacrilegious aural punning on "Domine" as he pleads for saving his belly: "Ma salvagli l'addomine."[56] The divine is brought down to earth—literally making the Word flesh—in the context of bodily rather than spiritual salvation. Ironic recontextualizing makes this less a simple echo than a complex secularizing parody of a religious gesture. Though the aging anticlerical Verdi would go on to complete the *Quattro pezzi sacri (Four Sacred Pieces)*, we wonder if this is not part of his last operatic laugh. In other words, it is not simply that "*Falstaff* holds within itself the whole of Verdi's past practice,"[57] but that these echoing links comment upon and support the drama in new ways. As Verdi himself wrote to a friend: "Let's go back to the old: it will be a step forward."[58]

But Verdi did not parody only himself in this last opera. George Bernard Shaw's review of the Covent Garden premiere of *Falstaff* in 1894 noted the fugue that ends the opera: it was, he said, "as if Verdi, in his old age, had clasped hands with Sebastian Bach."[59] But it was less often Bach than Beethoven and Mozart, Handel, Haydn, and Weber whose echoes have been noted, and most often noted of all, amid all this Germanic echoing, was Richard Wagner. For reasons that will become clear, the example that interests us here is Verdi's echoing parody of Wagner's own final opera, *Parsifal* (1882). When he was composing this last, very un-ironic work, Wagner (aware of negative judgments on aging artists who repeated themselves) expressed worries about his continuing originality, and so, like other members of his circle, he was always anxious about any echoes, especially of himself, that might creep into the opera.[60] The confident, experienced Verdi had no such worries about echoing himself or others, for he had a mission—and a sense of humor: his last opera's relative brevity, its short melodic lines, its seeming refusal to repeat melodies, and even its hectic pace can all be read as ironic comments upon the length of line, frequency of motivic repetition, stately slowness, and sheer length of *Parsifal*. Indeed, Roger Parker has shown how Verdi executes specific "ironic reversals" of Wagnerian compositional strategies, imagining the Italian to be saying that Wagner's "disciples abuse dissonances, I'll celebrate perfect triads; they indulge in constant slurs, I'll indulge in constant staccati."[61] Parker points out that the orchestral prelude to act 3 of *Falstaff* and Wagner's prelude to act 2 of *Parsifal* are both "obsessively concerned with repeated sixteenth-note patterns in the strings, but with the crucial difference that Verdi's is staccato and mostly diatonic, while Wagner's is legato and mostly chromatic."

FALSTAFF AS ITALIAN REMEDY FOR GERMANIC ILLS

Like *Falstaff, Parsifal* is a story of age and generational crisis, but the two operas' solutions to such a crisis could not be more different. In the years during which Wagner composed his last opera, he not only scrutinized himself for symptoms of decline in "inspiration, invention, and technical fluency,"[62] but had also become deeply concerned with what he saw as the degeneration (*Entartung*) of the entire human race. He believed he understood the causes of this: miscegenation, a nonvegetarian diet, vivisection and other forms of cruelty to animals, and hereditary wealth (supported by the state and the church). In his diaries and in a series of what are called the "regeneration" essays in the *Bayreuther Blätter* in the early 1880s, he both analyzed the problems and offered what he saw as solutions. Inspired in part by Joseph-Arthur de Gobineau's biologized theories of culture and race and Ernst Häckel's popularization of Darwinism, these essays are coeval with the final scoring and performing of *Parsifal*—the most problematic of his operas for his critics from Nietzsche to the present. However offensive Wagner's anti-Semitic regeneration writings are to today's readers, there can be no doubt that they are the conclusions of someone who saw himself as profoundly engaged in thinking about the future of the human race in a serious intellectual (if megalomaniac) way.

Wagner's last opera tells the story of the decline of a once noble society—the Grail realm—to whose leader the Holy Spear and Grail had been entrusted by God. Its narrative, following the passing on of responsibility by the now aged leader to his son, Amfortas, echoes the themes of Wagner's essays of the same time.[63] When Parsifal, the youth, is chastised for killing a swan, we are reminded of the essays against cruelty to animals. The more offensive writings on the corruption of the blood by the mixing of races and the need for the renunciation of the flesh seem incarnated in the portrayal of Kundry, an exoticized, sexualized, and Judaicized woman from the East who has caused the fall of Amfortas, the new Grail leader. That this fallen society can only be saved by someone from outside—Parsifal—who learns from his initial sin against nature and comes to experience suffering and compassion (*Mitleid*) for the wounded Amfortas is another of Wagner's firmly held, personal, individualist beliefs. So too is his assertion that art and religion together can redeem humankind from degeneration: *Parsifal* ends with the Christian communion ceremony performed by the redeeming Parsifal.

How very different is Wagner's story of decline, renunciation, and generational salvation from Boito and Verdi's rollicking *Falstaff*, the story of a corpulent, aging, but exuberantly sensual knight who seeks to fill his depleted purse by seducing two wealthy wives of Windsor. Thanks to the women's ingenuity and wit, they manage not only to outsmart Falstaff but also to teach Alice's jealous husband a lesson or two, including one about standing in the way of the young love of his daughter, Nannetta, and Fenton. In the process, the merry wives administer to Falstaff a number of humbling setbacks, the first of which involves his being tossed into the muddy waters of the Thames River out of a laundry basket in which he has been hiding. Immediately following this dunking, act 3 opens with the humiliated, soaking wet Falstaff lamenting his age and his size—to music that parodies, in a minor key, music we have already heard, but sung in a very smug, self-satisfied manner, in act 2, when he first learned of his success in obtaining an assignation with Alice Ford. In that earlier moment he had celebrated, not lamented, his large body, affectionately addressing himself as "old John" ("vecchio John"), old but eager and ready for another amorous adventure: "Questa tua vecchia carne ancora spreme / Qualche dolcezza a te" (This old flesh of yours can still wring out / Some sweetness for you).[64] Going on to address his "buon corpo di Sir John, ch'io nutro e sazio" (good body of Sir John, that I nourish and sate), he glories in his corpulent splendor, singing these lines to "strutting accompaniment on strings, bassoons, brass, and timpani" and with "a slow and splendidly self-satisfied four-in-a-bar."[65] The next time we hear that music, the context is very different. He repeats the words, but this time the now listless music and the minor key underline the fact that they are meant literally: he really does feel old and fat after his spill into the cold Thames waters ("Impinguo troppo. Ho dei peli grigi").[66] At this point a gloomy phrase appears in the strings, echoing directly a motif from *Parsifal* (see fig. 2). In Wagner's opera this motif is associated with magic and with the evil—and self-castrated—character named Klingsor who had helped bring about the decline of the Grail realm.[67] Given that we know that Verdi owned the Wagner score and had spent a lifetime worrying about the Germanism infecting Italian operatic production, it seems unlikely that this echo is an unconscious reminiscence or even a private joke, as some have suggested.[68] Sung after Falstaff's morose declaration that "Tutto declina" (All is in decline), the words to this music are "Che giornataccia nera. M'aiuti il ciel!"

PARSIFAL

Fig. 2. Richard Wagner, *Parsifal*, act 2, mm. 20–21

FALSTAFF

Fig. 3. Giovanni Verdi, *Falstaff*, act 3, part 1

(What a horrid black day. Heaven help me!) (see fig. 3).[69] Recognizing this intrusive chromatic motif in the middle of a sunny comedy can provoke in audience members an enlargement—through comic ironizing—of our interpretation of the stage business: the cold, wet Falstaff feels he too is now in a fallen world, one in which he has been (figuratively) unmanned by those merry wives.

While this is indeed a moment in which he looks at himself with "bleak honesty," as Roger Parker has argued,[70] it is a very fleeting one, quickly reversed by simple bodily pleasures. Unlike Wagner's renunciation of the flesh and his turn to the Christian communion, Verdi offers instead a very secular embracing of the sensual and a celebration of physical delights: Falstaff is completely restored with a cup of hot mulled wine. He revels in this sensuous pleasure: "Buono.—Ber del vin dolce e sbottonarsi al sole, / Dolce cosa!" (Good. To drink sweet wine and unbutton oneself in the sun, / A sweet thing!). Good wine, he insists, disperses all gloomy thoughts of discouragement ("le tetre fole / Dello sconforto"); it lights up the eye and sharpens the wit ("accende l'occhio e il pensier").[71] This physical celebration and the trilling exuberant music that accompanies it offer Dr. Verdi's very Italianate cure for Germanic psychic ills. Boito even used this image to describe the creator of *Falstaff*'s "regenerative therapy," writing to Verdi after the premiere: "You today are not only the Maestro: you are the Physician . . . the Physician of Art. Today Milan is entirely purged of any ultramontane fog"—a direct reference to the German Wagner.[72] And we know, from Verdi's frequent letters to Boito, that Wagner had been very much on his mind as he composed this particular part of the opera (the last to be orchestrated because it was "shorter, and less difficult than the others," according to Verdi).[73]

To add to the Italian jollity, the opera ends with a lively fugue—arguably another Germanic form appropriated (and Italianized) by Verdi. Here all the generations' voices merge harmoniously, creating a new aural as well as social community, now incorporating Falstaff, with whom they all go off to dinner ("E poi con Falstaff, tutti, andiamo a cena").[74] It begins with the seemingly cynical words "Tutto nel mondo è burla" (Everything in the world is a joke), because everyone is born a joker ("burlone"), fooled by both heart and his head. All are deceived: "tutti gabbati." But the fugue ends not with cynicism but with hearty laughter: "Ma ride ben chi ride / La risata final" (But he laughs well who laughs / The final laugh).[75] This high-spirited ending is what led Italy's major theorist of degeneration, Cesare Lombroso, to be amazed at Verdi's late creativity. Because Verdi was noticeably the liveliest person around during the rehearsals of *Falstaff*, the press had consulted Lombroso (who had once argued that artistic genius was an example of the degenerative—like the insane). But he found Verdi incomprehensible, at least in terms of his own theories. "The fact of a masterpiece like *Falstaff* created by an elderly man of eighty" was what he called an "extraordinary event," adding, "When I think that *Falstaff* is a totally merry and happy conception, and that in old age more gloomy notes usually prevail, . . . I confess that every possible explanation escapes me."[76]

Commentators have seen *Falstaff* both as different from all the operas that preceded it and yet also as a kind of culmination of them. All the composer's personal mannerisms—from structural details to instrumentation—are there. We find the same use of duets at the central point of the action, followed by the other great pivot in Verdi opera, the beautiful aria. There is the customary lack of vocal melisma and the usual seamless continuity of transitions. The delicate style of scoring comic moments is also typically Verdian.[77] The subject matter is no longer tragic death and national politics, and the genre is now comedy. But national aesthetic politics figure in a major way in Verdi's echoing responses, and self-parody allows him a way to offer a summation of his compositional career without fear of duplication. The fact that he does so in an opera whose narrative is about age and its sensual pleasures—rather than about abdication of responsibility, death, and the renunciation of the flesh (as in *Parsifal* or, had Verdi completed it, *Re Lear*)—suggests that the appeal of Boito's libretto for the aging Verdi lay not only in its wit. And ending the opera with the Germanic fugue, in order both formally and aurally to integrate Falstaff into the community of Windsor, means not only once again commenting on the German tradition, but also using it for his own musical ends.

THE LAST YEARS, THE FINAL LEGACY

The opening words of that fugue—though they are Boito's—obviously resonated with Verdi, for he repeated them often in his letters at the time and after: "tutto nel mondo è burla" (everything in the world is a joke). The seeming cynicism of these words has to be tempered by the vocal fellowship of the fugue and with that physical celebration of community at the end of the opera. The admittedly pessimistic Verdi used this joking line as a mantra, as a sign of his way of perceiving the trials of life, especially as he aged. The only possible response was Falstaff's "Va', vecchio John, va', va' per la tua via finché tu puoi" (Go, go, old John . . . Go on your way as long as you can).[78] Writing to the singer who premiered Falstaff, Victor Maurel, about a disagreement, the composer ended his letter with: "Now I'm a bit of a skeptic, I laugh and laugh! It's true, though, that not everyone's lucky enough to be eighty years old!! *Va! va! vecchio John per la tua via*, and don't worry about anything else."[79]

Verdi's last years were not as easy as these words might suggest. As he aged into "old old age" in his later eighties, he experienced the loss of his wife and his own increased physical frailty. As he put it: "I have felt the weight of age!"[80] He wrote to a close friend: "Oh an old man's life is truly unhappy! Even without real illness, life is a burden, and I feel that vitality and strength are diminishing, each day more than the one before. I feel this within myself and I don't have the courage and power to keep busy with anything."[81] He marked each of his birthdays with letters lamenting his advancing age and complaining about problems with mobility, eyesight, and hearing.[82] And just days before his death at the age of eighty-eight, he wrote: "I can no longer read, nor write; my eyes are giving out; my feeling dims; and even my legs don't want to carry me around anymore. Why am I still in this world?"[83]

Verdi would leave more than his operas as his legacy to Italy. In his last years, once he became financially secure, Verdi began building a series of philanthropic establishments. In 1888 he constructed a hospital for poor farmworkers and their families in a village near his farm. In Milan today, there still stands a Casa di Riposo for elderly musicians that Verdi founded late in his life and where he and his wife are now buried.

But his lasting *musical* message, beyond the many operas themselves, also includes that prolonged resistance to Wagner's influence on the young. Despite what he lamented as his failed attempts at stopping the Teutonic invasion in musical education through the reform of the Italian conservatory system after unification, he still thought he could *show* the way.[84] Even the *scapigliato* Boito became convinced of the need to preserve the Italian past: "I believe that in our conservatories it . . . should be *compulsory* to study Palestrina and the other Italian master musicians of the sixteenth, seventeenth, and eighteenth centuries. That is the right path," he wrote to Verdi in 1887.[85] In their parodic *Falstaff* Verdi not only distanced himself, through irony, from the Germanism he saw as debilitating to that Italian tradition. He also offered the next generation of composers a positive example of a new alternative, something distinctly Italian yet new at the same time. This is Verdi's other operatic legacy, one that explains both continuity and change in his last work and in his late style. The desire to preserve tradition while simultaneously nurturing the next generation is a definition of generativity, a goal for older age;[86] but Verdi went beyond saving the tradition: he recognized that it had to change with the times but remain Italian nonetheless.

Given that Verdi's last and overtly didactic opera was widely performed and well-known, did the younger composers pay any heed? Giacomo Puccini (1858–1924), considered by many to be Verdi's heir apparent, was at the premiere of *Falstaff* as the guest of Giulio Ricordi, who was also *his* publisher. While the younger composer's early operas, such as *Le villi* (1884) and *Manon Lescaut* (1894), demonstrated an overt debt to Wagner, surely the verbal and musical energy of *Gianni Schicchi* (1918), Puccini's only comedy, not to mention that of the first scene of *La bohème* (1896), were deeply indebted to *Falstaff*. Other composers were also impressed and influenced by Verdi's message. Ermanno Wolf-Ferrari (1876–1948) has most often been seen as the comic inheritor of Verdi's late treasure, with his *Segreto di Susanna* (1909) and other musical comedies. But the impact extended even further. Witness the extant but unsent letter to Verdi from Ferruccio Busoni (1866–1924): "*Falstaff* provoked such a complete spiritual and emotional upheaval, that I can honestly say it marked the beginning of a new era in my life as an artist."[87] And in England, Britten later gave a copy of *Falstaff* to Eric Crozier, the librettist of his comedy *Albert Herring*, considering it "the most perfect of its kind."[88]

Whether we see it as irony or revenge (or both), it may have been a younger German who would learn Verdi's Italian lesson best of all: Richard Strauss, for whom Verdi's last work was one of the masterpieces of music, sent a copy of his first opera, *Guntram*, to the elderly Verdi by way of homage. Strauss's later operas, such as *Der Rosenkavalier* (1911), *Ariadne auf Naxos* (1916), and *Intermezzo* (1926), brought to the German operatic stage the new kind of comedy that Verdi had told Ricordi he had invented, with its "rapid flow of dialogue" and comic brio.

But something else was happening in the music world at the end of the nineteenth century that would affect the reception of both the older Verdi himself and these younger successors: the advent of cultural modernity and musical modernism. This new ideology would make a different set of demands on composers. As Alexandra Wilson has so convincingly argued, modernity and tradition turned out to be "structurally incompatible" in Italy.[89] In the next chapter we shall see that the impact of both modernity and modernism would be felt not just in Italy but across Europe, including in the Germany of Richard Strauss.

CHAPTER FOUR

Richard Strauss (1864–1949):
A Life Review in Music

As the conduit through which our past is channeled to the present, the
aged are of critical importance to society, at least to the one that wants
to remember its past.
—James J. Dowd, "The Old Person as Stranger"

In 1900 the thirty-six-year-old Richard Strauss bravely defended Verdi's
Falstaff against the accusation of the German Kaiser Wilhelm II that
the Italian's last opera was a "detestable thing." "Your Majesty," he pro-
tested, "one must bear in mind that Verdi is eighty years old, and it is a
splendid thing, after having created *Il trovatore* and *Aida*, to renew oneself
again at the age of eighty, to create a work like *Falstaff*, which has genius
in it." The kaiser simply replied: "I hope that when you're eighty you'll
write better music."[1]

As it happened, when Strauss himself turned eighty, he had just finished what would be his own last operatic work, *Capriccio*, a neobaroque
opera about . . . opera. The trouble was that this work premiered in Munich in 1942, in the middle of World War II. To later critics, any decision
about whether this work might or might not be superior to Verdi's was pre-
empted by its seeming inappropriateness or even triviality in the historical context of the moment. The last two decades of Strauss's life—he died
in 1949 at the age of eighty-five—were deeply troubled years for Germany,
with the rise of National Socialism, the war, and its aftermath. The reception of Strauss's work has been inseparable from his own problematic relationship to the historical events of these years, as we shall see. However,
we want to argue that the last works must also be considered in relation
not just to this political history but also to his *creative* history as a specifically German composer writing at a time when music was changing radi-

cally. His entire sense of himself as an artist depended upon this context. His broader sense of himself as a person, however, came from his family. The fact that both of these—his musical reputation and members of his immediate family—came under threat in the last decades of his life must be taken into account in considering the late works.

CAREER NARRATIVES VERSUS CREATIVITY NARRATIVES

However varied their positions on his political involvement, the many biographies of Strauss all construct a life narrative of a child prodigy who rose to national and international fame through his tone poems before switching to opera in his thirties.[2] The subsequent story they all tell is a familiar artistic one of a creative rise followed by decline, yet ending with a glorious Indian summer. The difficulty is that there is little agreement on where either the decline or the Indian summer actually begins. For some, his genius starts to fade as early as 1911 with *Der Rosenkavalier*, when he left behind the modernist experimentation of *Salome* and *Elektra*;[3] for others, it is in 1929, with the death of Hugo von Hofmannsthal, his librettist for twenty years.[4] In a similarly confusing fashion, in some of these narratives, the redeeming Indian summer is said to begin as early as *Daphne* or *Die Liebe der Danae*, that is, in the mid- to late 1930s;[5] in others, it is only with his appropriately labeled *Vier letzte Lieder* (*Four Last Songs*)—in other words, at the very end of his life in the late 1940s. But these are all *career* narratives, not necessarily narratives about *creativity*.

If an artist were to continue working as productively and consistently as Strauss did, he or she would certainly be continuing to be creative. The conflicting evaluations and disagreements over the quality of the last works may have more to do with other things than the compositions themselves. It is no accident, in other words, that those various suggested dates of decline are coincident with either musical modernism's ascendency or Strauss's complicated involvement with the National Socialist regime. Musically, Strauss continued to compose, essentially using the same harmonic and melodic language he always had—and that was precisely the problem for anyone assessing the work from the perspective of musical modernism. Politically, his fraught interactions with the government were open to the interpretation of complicity and therefore to censure. In creative terms, however, Strauss matured early and continued to be "Strauss" throughout his later life.[6]

By the age of thirty-four Strauss had both made his name as a conductor and had also written those tone poems that had established his international reputation. When he then turned to opera, as we have seen, he dedicated his first effort, *Guntram* (1894), to Verdi, writing to him: "I can find no words to describe the impression made on me by the extraordinary beauty of *Falstaff*. Consider my dedication as thanks for this reawakening of your genius."[7] But both *Guntram*, for which he had served as his own librettist, and his next effort, *Feuersnot* (1901), for which he trusted a friend's libretto, were not really successes, in part because of their texts. He himself always admitted that he needed to be inspired by words before he could write music for them. It was only in 1905, with *Salome*, that he found the right libretto and made his mark as an opera composer. His adaptation of Hedwig Lachmann's translation of Oscar Wilde's sensational play *Salomé* was a smash hit. Strauss's dramatic use of musical dissonance, chromaticism, and even tonal ambiguity in this work was a major musical shift for him, one he would extend even further in his next opera, an adaptation of Hofmannsthal's play *Elektra* (1909). This turned out to be Strauss's brief moment of avant-garde glory, especially in the eyes of those viewing the work later through the lenses of a dominant modernist aesthetic: Theodor Adorno asserted that one "seemingly wildly pieced-together" scene in it "probably marks a high point he never again equaled."[8] The opera's daring musical score was considered cutting-edge and seen by some as the height of Strauss's creativity. It was new; it was progressive. Modernist ideology heartily approved of these two early operas of Strauss—not for their manifest craft, but for their musical and dramatic novelty.

While *Elektra* marked the beginning of a long and fruitful collaboration with the Austrian Hofmannsthal, the librettist he had been looking for, it also led to a major change—but not in the right direction, at least for modernist ears. Much to the critics' dismay and the general public's delight, the pair's new opera, *Der Rosenkavalier* (1911), did not continue in the radical vein (musically or dramatically) of the last two but instead moved back to the eighteenth century in its subject matter and to a more traditional musical style. Over the next twenty years Strauss and Hofmannsthal would continue in this same manner, together creating *Ariadne auf Naxos* (1916), *Die Frau ohne Schatten* (1919), *Die ägyptische Helena* (1928), and *Arabella*. The last was composed between 1929 and 1932 but did not premiere until 1933, four years after the librettist's sudden death at the age of fifty-five.

Losing Hofmannsthal led to a crisis in the composer's life. He himself was sixty-five years old at the time, an age that was officially deemed elderly in the Germany of those years. (In 1889 the chancellor, Otto von

Bismarck, had created the first old-age pension system for industrial and agrarian workers, artisans, and servants; his designation of the pensionable age as sixty-five at a time when the life expectancy of Prussians was forty-five meant that sixty-five was definitely a marker of "old age" in the German public's eye.) However, at this point in his life, Strauss was still the most prominent living German composer and had absolutely no intention of stopping composing. But he knew from experience that he needed a librettist—a good one.[9] The year was 1929, and the Germany he had known all his life was changing rapidly: the National Socialists were already a political force to be reckoned with, and by 1933 Hitler would be in power. But in the career narrative of many postwar critics, Hofmannsthal's death marks the beginning of Strauss's artistic "decline." As one put it strongly in 1967, "His decline was precipitous and prolonged, so precipitous indeed that his case is almost unique in the history of music."[10] However, the reasons for this judgment have less to do with the quality of the work Strauss produced from then on than with his perceived role in the musical life of Germany during the Nazi regime.

THE NATIONAL SOCIALIST YEARS

In 1933 a very complicated relationship between the composer and the National Socialists began. Strauss accepted the invitation to be the president of the government's newly founded musical oversight body, the Reichsmusikkammer. He had high, if naive (and perhaps opportunistic), hopes that the German nationalism espoused by the Nazis could be of benefit to German art, especially to German composers like himself. A year later he would write: "I have, in fact, been able to accomplish some fruitful things and prevent some misfortune."[11] The truth was that, while no innocent, and deeply contemptuous about politics in general,[12] Strauss seems to have filtered what he saw happening around him in Germany through a complex mixture of arrogance, self-interest, idealism, and as events progressed, the need to protect his family. In the same year that he accepted the presidency, a year during which laws forbidding Jews to hold positions in musical organizations were enacted by the regime, Strauss also agreed to replace the Jewish conductor Bruno Walter in a concert in March 1933 with the Philharmonic Orchestra in Berlin—for the good of the orchestra, he said. Since he also stepped in that year when the antifascist Arturo Toscanini quit the Bayreuth Festival in protest, Strauss was inevitably seen as complicit with the Nazis.

These were the same years in which Strauss was casting about desperately for a new librettist. His first choice was the well-known Austrian writer Stefan Zweig, with whom he went on to create *Die schweigsame Frau*, which premiered in 1935. Strauss's refusal to obey the Nazi edict and take the Jewish Zweig's name off the program and publicity materials led to the abrupt closing of the piece after only four performances. Zweig, more politically astute, perhaps, than Strauss, then said that he would no longer collaborate publicly with the composer, both to protect Strauss's (and his own) reputation and in solidarity with other banned Jewish artists.[13] In a passionate attempt to dissuade him from withdrawing, Strauss wrote a strong letter to Zweig attacking the Nazis' anti-Semitic policies. Unfortunately for both, the Gestapo intercepted the letter.[14] As a result, Strauss was immediately relieved of the Reichsmusikkammer presidency. Though he was now persona non grata in the eyes of the regime, he nevertheless was still the foremost (and most performed) living German composer, so the Nazis continued to use him as a public figure whenever it suited them.[15] And Strauss allowed himself to be used, in part so that his works would continue to be performed, and in part, as we shall see, for family reasons. But he was never a Nazi or an anti-Semite. In 1935 he wrote in his notebooks that he considered the "Jew baiting" of the Reich Minister of Public Enlightenment and Propaganda, Joseph Goebbels, as "a disgrace to German honor, as evidence of incompetence, the basest weapon of untalented, lazy mediocrity against a higher intelligence and greater talent."[16] Although Strauss agreed to compose and conduct the *Olympische Hymne* for the 1936 Berlin Olympics, Goebbels tellingly wrote in his diary at this time: "Unfortunately we still need him, but one day we shall have our own music and then we shall have no further need of this decadent neurotic."[17]

Strauss's professional woes during the 1930s continued on other fronts. He had written to Zweig that, if he abandoned the composer, Strauss would have to "lead from now on the life of an ailing, unemployed retiree."[18] Yet he did find another librettist, though the match was never a good one. With the theater historian Josef Gregor he created *Friedenstag*, which premiered in 1938. After considerable initial success, this too was shelved by the Nazis after war broke out, in this case because of its pacifist message. Strauss's family situation also changed dramatically in these years, and for a man whose sense of personhood was based not only in his work but also in his family, this was the beginning of an extremely difficult time. His Jewish daughter-in-law, Alice, and therefore his two beloved grandsons, came under threat. Strauss actively worked on their behalf, sometimes writing sycophantic letters to the Nazi authorities that make the modern reader cringe. On Kristallnacht, 9–10 November 1938, an arrest warrant was issued for Alice, but she was away, hidden in a Düsseldorf clinic. Upon her return to the Strauss home in Garmisch-Partenkirchen, she was put under curfew and her personal papers were confiscated. On that same Kristallnacht, Strauss's two grandsons were beaten up, taken to the public square, and forced to spit upon Jews who had been gathered there.[19] The threat to the safety of his family was a real one and would preoccupy the composer until the end of the war.

Yet Strauss continued to compose. His next, not entirely happy collaborations with Gregor yielded *Daphne*, which also premiered in 1938, and *Die Liebe der Danae*. The outline for this latter opera had been drafted by Hofmannsthal back in 1920, but Strauss composed the music between 1938 and 1940. He was determined to withhold it from production until after the war, but in 1944 he was persuaded by the conductor Clemens Krauss to permit its premiere at the Salzburg Festival in celebration of the composer's eightieth birthday. However, before that could take place, Goebbels ordered the closure of all festivals, and specifically the one in Salzburg, and so only one dress rehearsal of the opera was allowed. Then the theaters of the German states were closed by order of the government.

MODERNISM AND THE RECEPTION
OF THE LATE WORKS

None of these late operatic works have found a secure place in the standard repertoire, and their timing is obviously in part to blame. While the operas composed before these were already popular with the public, the historical moment and the composer's political disfavor muted any impact they could have had at the time of their composition and premiere. None got much play at all. While *Daphne* has recently come to be more accepted, there is another reason for the later mustering of these works in evidence of Strauss's "decline": they had not changed. They were not innovative, and they certainly were not considered modernist. Strauss was still the consummate craftsman and traditionalist he had always been (except for the *Salome/Elektra* moment)—and that was the problem. Given the ideology of modernism that academic postwar music critics consciously or unconsciously adopted, not to change—not to progress—was tantamount to decline. As Ezra Pound memorably and canonically put that ideology: "Make it new." Strauss did not. In a modernist musical climate heavily influenced by the work of the Second Viennese School (whose avant-garde credentials were assured by their being banned by the Nazis as degener-

ate), Strauss was out of musicological fashion (though not public appreciation). As early as 1914 Arnold Schoenberg had written of Strauss: "He is no
longer of the slightest artistic interest to me, and whatever I might once
have learned from him, I am thankful to say I have misunderstood. . . . I
have inwardly rejected Strauss."[20] While Strauss too deliberately recalled
earlier musical periods in his operas, this practice had very little in common with Stravinsky's contemporaneous neo-classical form of modernism
either. The composer of *Salome* and *Elektra* had once been considered radical, but for the next thirty years he had "regressed" in modernist eyes. In
the 1920s "Strauss had generally been written off by influential critics in
Germany, Britain and America as no longer a composer holding out any
progressive interest. He belonged to the past."[21]

In short, Strauss simply remained Strauss; but the musical world
changed, and Strauss did not like the changes, scorning the avant-garde
experimentation that surrounded him. As early as 1911 he saw the direction in which Schoenberg was heading and wrote: "I think he'd do better
to shovel snow instead of scribbling on music-paper." But this wasn't simply a single attack on a younger composer whom he had once supported:
he once asked Paul Hindemith why he wrote atonally when he had real
talent.[22]

Strauss's unaltering persistence made him seem to some "an extinct
volcano, an arch-conservative living off his own fat, composing by numbers"[23]—and that meant decline, the "fading of his genius into a combination of talent and technique."[24] But talent and technique should not, perhaps, be written off quite so readily: indeed, following in the footsteps of
Glenn Gould, Edward W. Said has argued that Strauss defies any existing
models of historical evolution in his continuing virtuosity. Said felt that
Strauss's late works offered "a third revision of the tonal system" after
Wagner and Schoenberg.[25] But Strauss, again, in a way just went on being
Strauss—which for him meant being an important (and consistent) composer continuing the long German musical tradition he venerated.[26] No
anguished modernist, no poor but passionate bohemian artist, the bourgeois, business-savvy composer was out of step with the times.[27]

THE MUSICAL LIFE REVIEW, PART I: *CAPRICCIO*

By the opening years of World War II, then, things had begun to go badly
for Strauss personally and politically. In that light, what are we to make of
his next work, the opera about opera, *Capriccio*? Strauss composed it in his
late seventies, in the middle of a war he could not ignore. For precisely this

reason—its timing—it is a work that has been seen by many as escapist. But it is also possible that, given his difficult professional and life circumstances in 1940–41, the increasingly isolated Strauss deliberately chose to begin something very inward-looking and personal, and perhaps very necessary at this point—in effect, an ongoing, retrospective artistic "life review" of his career as a composer. Here we want to adapt the concept of the life review, first outlined by Robert Butler in 1963 as the practice of older people who, through active reminiscence, come to evaluate their lives as a whole as a way of achieving psychic reintegration.[28] We want to suggest, instead, an artistic (rather than psychological) version of that practice whereby the older composer engages in compositional memory work in order to review and assess his artistic legacy. In this way, both the continuities of his late work with what came before *and* the great variety of genres and moods of the late music that he composed in his last years can be accounted for, without falling into the contradictorily evaluative traps of biographical career models of either decline or Indian summer. With *Capriccio*, it was his operatic career in particular that would come under review in this new operatic genre, which he called a *Konversationsstück für Musik* (conversation piece for music)—that is, a very theoretically self-conscious work of antitheater on the topic of the nature of opera itself.[29] This was the culmination of Strauss's Verdian experiments, which had begun in the Prologue of *Ariadne auf Naxos*, to develop a new conversational style somewhere between aria and recitative, one that has been seen as his major contribution to the art of opera.[30]

Developed with the aid of the conductor Clemens Krauss, the opera's eighteenth-century plot, such as it is, centers around that century's particular question,[31] one that still obsessed Strauss: which is most important to the art form—words or music? Set outside Paris in 1777, just before the French Revolution was to overthrow the ancien régime, it tells the story of the Countess Madeleine, who is being courted by the poet Olivier and the composer Flamand, both seeking to win her love with their respective arts. With the impresario and director LaRoche, the guardian of theatrical tradition, drama enters the words/music debate. This is a very "talky" opera: these three characters open the work with an extended debate about the value of specific composers and librettists. This theme is then picked up by the Countess and her brother when they enter. It is not hard to see what this discussion is really about: this is what Strauss himself thought about opera and its history. And LaRoche's views certainly echo those of Strauss, beset by the changes he too lamented in the new avant-garde music of modernism: "Ich bewahre das Gute, das wir besitzen, / die Kunst unsrer Väter halte ich hoch. / Voll Pietät hüte ich das Alte" (I preserve the good that is ours, / hold high the art of our fathers. / Reverently I preserve the old).[32] Like the older Strauss, perhaps, all LaRoche sees around him are "blasse Ästheten" (pale aesthetes) who ridicule the old but create nothing new: "Die heutige Jugend— / sie hat keine Ehrfurcht! / . . . Einer trostlosen Zukunft / gehen sie entgegen! / Lachend—in ihrem Unverstand!" (Present-day youth—they have no respect. They are heading for a hopeless future. Laughing—in their ignorance!).[33] We can also see the composer's own views echoed in the defense of music as the language of the soul, voiced by the Countess.[34] As she articulates music's power: "Dunkle Träume wecken sie—unaussprechlich— / Ein Meer von Empfindingung— beglückend schön!" (It awakens dark dreams—ineffable— / A sea of awareness—entrancingly beautiful!).[35]

One of the amusing things about the opera's self-reflexivity is that despite the seemingly unoperatic nature of the characters' long and trenchant critique of the excesses of Italian opera and praise of Gluck's corrective operatic reforms, their debate about music, poetry, and drama ends with the Countess commissioning a three-way collaboration in the form of an opera on this very topic. And, of course, it will be the opera we are witnessing. We already know that neither the composer nor the poet will win the love of the Countess; neither music nor words will triumph. The Countess prefigured this result early in the piece when she said that making such a choice would mean only loss ("denn hier zu wählen, hiesse verlieren"). For her, words make music, and music speaks: "Worte klingen, Töne sprechen."[36]

Strauss's musical life review does not only take place in the opera's story line, however. It also occurs in the music itself, for the composer quotes himself throughout the piece. When possible subjects for the birthday celebration work are discussed, those of earlier Strauss operas are mentioned, such as *Ariadne auf Naxos* and *Daphne*—and the orchestra duly and not un-ironically quotes them.[37] But here, in this most self-conscious of works, Strauss is citing himself in the context of quotations from other *opera* composers: Gluck, Piccinni, Rameau, Rossini, Donizetti, Verdi, and Wagner—that is, in the context of a major operatic tradition.[38] Strauss had always indulged in quoting himself, as well as many other composers, and he did so especially in works that were autobiographical in some way or that he (or others) saw as summational: the last tone poem, *Ein Heldenleben* (1899), where he cited all but one of his preceding tone poems,[39] and the very personal *Sinfonia Domestica* (1904) and *Intermezzo* (1926), among others.[40] Like these works, *Capriccio* is as close as Strauss ever came to achieving what he told Hofmannsthal he had always wanted to do: "to put myself to music."[41] Not merely citational, these references represent, within their new setting, a placing of himself and his music (self-consciously and often ironically) within the specific context of other opera composers and their works. Rather than seeing such references as anachronistic, archaic, or nostalgic,[42] therefore, we see them as part of his musical life review process, undertaken at a particularly vulnerable moment in his late life. If, as one critic negatively put it, "shadowy ghosts of phrases from earlier Strauss stage works stalk the music,"[43] they stalk with a purpose: the review of a life's work in the specific genre of opera.

As mentioned earlier, this opera about opera has been seen as escapist, as out of tune with the times—the war years, during which it was written and first performed—though it is also true that it was very well received by the public at the time.[44] It may be escapist,[45] but we also see it as part of the older composer's reviewing and affirming his position on the complexity of the art form he had been engaged with for over forty years. He thought the end of the opera was "the best conclusion of my life's theatrical work," adding: "One can, after all, only leave *one* last will and testament."[46] Strauss's sense of personhood was deeply bound up with his identity as a composer—and therefore with his reputation and his position within the German musical tradition. For some critics, this was a form of *Kunstegoismus*—artistic egoism—that would make him indifferent (or naive) to all kinds of politics, even during the war.[47] As what Michael Kater has called an "aesthetocrat," Strauss cared mostly about art, especially *his* art. *Capriccio* was certainly deeply introspective and personal. He later wrote to Krauss, who had been both his librettist and the conductor of the Munich premiere, that he considered this to be his *Schluss*, the good and worthy end of a long operatic career.[48] Many have agreed, seeing it (as they had Verdi's *Falstaff*) as a "recapitulation, a summation, a farewell."[49]

A farewell to opera, perhaps; but not to music, for Strauss would continue to compose. He did finish *Capriccio* at the same age Verdi was when he completed his last opera, and not surprisingly, given Strauss's admiration of Verdi's late work, *Capriccio* has tangible links to the Italian composer that are more than historical accident. For example, one of the German opera's last lines echoes Verdi's final fugue on the words "Tutto nel mondo è burla" (Everything in the world is a joke): "Die ganze Welt ist närrisch" (The whole world is foolish)—to which the librettists add, "alles spielt Theater" (all play at theater).[50] When Strauss began composing the opera, he wrote to Krauss that he wanted to write a theatrical fugue (and he would), because even "the good Verdi" couldn't resist writing one.[51] But it was also the critics and biographers who could not resist linking the late Verdi and the late Strauss, either in their seeming rejuvenation at almost eighty or in what was considered their "serene detachment" and thus their last operas' perceived "mixture of exhilaration and unbearable poignancy."[52]

PERSONHOOD UNDER THREAT

Verdi's last years were rather different from Strauss's, however. The Nazi threat to Strauss's daughter-in-law continued, though he did manage to have his grandsons exempted from having their passports stamped with their Jewish identity. Alice, however, was refused any such exemption from the Nuremberg Racial Laws. In 1943 she and Strauss's son, Franz, were arrested in Vienna and questioned. Thanks to Strauss's efforts and with the intervention of a number of people, including the Nazi governor, Baldur von Schirach—the son of a theater director and composer—they were set free. Back in Garmisch-Partenkirchen, another warrant for Alice's arrest was issued in 1944 but was never served. Her family was not so fortunate: many did not survive the war, despite Strauss's personal attempt to intervene at the Theresienstadt concentration camp. There is no doubt that in these years Strauss frequently relied for protection and assistance in dealing with the regime upon his personal connections with high-ranking Nazis, such as Schirach and another longtime admirer, Hans Frank, the infamous governor of Poland who would be condemned to death at the Nuremberg trials.

When Strauss turned eighty in June 1944, there were very few of the official German celebrations that had greeted his seventieth birthday, before he fell out of favor with the Nazis. A few months later, when Goebbels formally closed all the theaters, Strauss wrote: "My life's work is in ruins. I shall never again hear my operas."[53] The blow to his sense of personhood that this realization meant was likely one of the major contributing causes to the depression into which Strauss then fell. The terrible destruction of the Allied bombing raids on Germany in these years brought home to Strauss the ruin of his beloved German culture, symbolized by the physical loss of the German and Austrian opera houses. When the Munich Nationaltheater was hit, Strauss wrote to a friend: "There is no consolation and, at my age, no hope."[54]

Obviously Strauss's stated motivations and activities—things that reveal, for us, at least part of his sense of personhood—were even more inwardly focused during his depression. His identification with his role as the provider for his family was almost as strong as his professional identity. With the theaters closed and his operas not being performed, his personal economic situation worsened. But he was also a compulsive worker and had always despaired when he did not have a new project in hand. One thing he did to keep himself occupied and, as he said, to keep himself from thinking about other things was to copy out old scores in order to provide sellable articles for his family's financial security.[55] Adding to these economic, professional, and political family worries were concerns for his physical health as he aged. His letters attest to problems with hearing and eyesight. Having given up smoking only at the age of seventy-five, he was "audibly asthmatic,"[56] we are told. But as a composer, though depressed, he continued to work, writing a goodly number of pieces in these years.

THE MUSICAL LIFE REVIEW, PART II:
THE FINAL WORKS

His continuing musical life review process may have been another reason for this continuing creativity. Revealingly, after the operatic summation that was *Capriccio*, Strauss went back to composing in forms he had not visited since his youth, writing, for example, two sonatinas for winds in 1943–45. His Second Horn Concerto of 1942 followed the one he had composed for his father to play back in 1882–83; it was even written in the same key (E-flat). Later critics would see in this work a revivification of the composer's talent. "In sheer youthfulness," wrote one, "it is hardly less remarkable than Verdi's *Falstaff*," finding it hard to believe that it was composed by "a depressed old man living in fear and disgrace from the authorities of a war-beleaguered country."[57] In fact, Strauss was simply continuing to be Strauss, and simply resuming his musical life review. To some, however, this meant that while still, in his old age, able to manipulate the concerto form with "ease and originality," he nevertheless belonged to a bygone era.[58]

But this musical critique was not the only kind of attack Strauss had to face in these years. What some see as a kind of return to the tone poem, *Metamorphosen*, a movingly mournful piece for twenty-three solo strings, would turn out to be the most politically problematic of these late works.[59] Written at the end of the war as a commission for the Zurich Collegium Musicum, it has been read by some as program music because of both its citation (or transformation) of a measure of the funeral march from Beethoven's *Eroica* Symphony and the inscription under it, "In Memoriam." However, seen as another part of Strauss's musical life review, *Metamorphosen* is an elegiac recollection of his own earlier work—with its citations of *Also sprach Zarathustra, Ariadne auf Naxos,* and *Feuers-not*[60]—as well as a meditation on the musical tradition out of which it came, signaled here by quotations from not only Beethoven but also Wagner.[61] As with *Capriccio,* his own works are not simply cited here; this time the references are situated or embedded in that larger German musical context in which Strauss felt his works belonged. Though his words are intended as a critique, Michael P. Steinberg is right when he says: "The work is about the past and about what kind of perspective on the past one's sense of history provides."[62] The title points to the role this piece plays in Strauss's life review: it comes from a poem in Goethe's *Zahme Xenien,* which Strauss wrote out in full amongst the pages of sketches for the piece. Goethe used the term *Metamorphosen* "in his old age when he contemplated works which had occupied his mind for a long period of time and compared them with the evolution of plant life, with seed growing into full flower, dying and reverting to seed."[63] But the composer of *Daphne* would also have had Ovid's *Metamorphoses* in mind, with all their mythological transformations, which had always fascinated him.

As Strauss's musical life review continued and the composer kept returning to his compositional roots, his critics noted something new that they found in his work, something they did not hesitate to call his late style: a reduced orchestration and therefore a new transparency, a chamber-music effect that made it all sound more Mozartian than (the usual) Wagnerian.[64] For some this was a refinement; for others it signaled a kind of musical shrinkage or shriveling.[65] What all agree on, however, is that his last works are characterized not by new or bold invention but rather by the "wise exploitation of all his creative experiences."[66] In other words, once again, Strauss continued to be Strauss.

DEPRESSION AND CREATIVITY

In the last months of the war the Strauss family returned to Garmisch-Partenkirchen to escape the bombing in Vienna. With the armistice and the arrival of American troops in Garmisch came both positive and negative new encounters. One of the soldiers to arrive at Strauss's door was John de Lancie, oboist in the Pittsburgh Symphony Orchestra, for whom Strauss would go on to write his Oboe Concerto. He was also visited and interviewed by a certain Mr. Brown. In reality, "Mr. Brown" was the son of Thomas Mann, Klaus Mann, who had never forgotten (or forgiven) that Strauss had signed the declaration of protest against his father's 1933 speech on Wagner as "un-German"—a document that convinced the writer to leave Germany. Klaus Mann's subsequent publications about this encounter did much to vilify Strauss in American eyes. Accompanied by a photo of the elderly composer with the caption "His heart beat in Nazi time" and describing him as "an old opportunist who heiled Hitler," the first article, which appeared on 29 May 1945 in the American forces publication *Stars and Stripes*, insisted that Strauss was not the least bit senile and went on to portray him throughout as a "selfish old man" who was thoroughly compromised by his association with the National Socialists. Mann's longer article in *Esquire* in January 1946 was even more condescending and condemning: "If it hadn't been for the master's age, I might have told him a few nasty things," he wrote. Finding Strauss "shockingly selfish and naïve," he labels him a "genius without any moral consciousness."[67] Needless to say, the personal and political complexities of the elderly composer's decision to stay in Germany during the war years were never taken into account.

This blow to Strauss's reputation was yet another of the pressures on his sense of personhood during the early postwar years. Whereas he had once suffered disfavor under the National Socialist regime, he was now being called a Nazi and would be subjected to intense scrutiny and critique until his denazification trial in 1948. Released from one set of worries about his family by the end of the war, he now had to face an entirely new set, with his integrity under attack and his economic situation worsening. His assets were frozen and his royalties appropriated by the Allied Property Control; there were to be no new performances of his work in the defeated countries. In October 1945 he and his wife left their increasingly hard postwar existence in Garmisch for Switzerland, but their arrival in that country was attacked in the anti-German Swiss press. Since the elderly couple had no money, a large number of Strauss's scores were put into the hotel safe as security against payment of the bill; they had to be assisted financially by his publisher in order to survive. Despite these distractions and his continuing depression, the workaholic Strauss continued to compose in these years—and thus continued his musical life review, now adapting his earlier operatic and ballet works into the *Rosenkavalier Suite* (1945), the *Capriccio Suite for Keyboard* (1946), and the *Fantasia from "Die Frau ohne Schatten"* (1946). What has been seen as his "generally retrospective outlook" at this time is arguably both a part of his life review process and an economic necessity:[68] while his operas may not have been able to be performed, perhaps shorter orchestral versions of them would and could be.

Strauss consistently downplayed the artistic importance of his late works after the testament and *Schluss* of *Capriccio*, writing to a friend: "The music that I go on scribbling for the benefit of my heirs, exercises for my wrists . . . has no significance whatsoever from the standpoint of musical history. . . . I do it only to dispel the boredom of idle hours."[69] The much-praised Second Horn Concerto, for instance, is what he called, in a letter to Karl Böhm, *Späne aus der Alterswerkstatt*—shavings from the old-age workshop.[70] This denigration of his "wrist exercises" might, however, be yet another sign of his ongoing depression at the time. Even in October 1947, when invited to England for a festival of his works, Strauss could only respond to a reporter who asked him what he was going to do next with the phlegmatic "Well, die."[71] Even the musical and financial success of the London trip did not lift his spirits, as he returned to face those official denazification hearings triggered by his two years as president of the Reichsmusikkammer.

The year 1947 also marked another politically motivated blow to Strauss's reputation when a Dutch newspaper attacked him on the occasion of the Amsterdam premiere of *Metamorphosen*. Since Beethoven had intended to dedicate his *Eroica* Symphony to Napoleon (before his disillusionment with him), Strauss's brief echoing of the funeral march from it was also read politically, as was his handwritten inscription under it of "In Memoriam": these were interpreted as a personal mourning of the end of Hitler and the Nazi regime. This article was reprinted in Switzerland and circulated widely, to the detriment of Strauss's reputation. Many came to his defense, however, arguing, very differently, that the Beethoven echo and the "In Memoriam" signaled the composer's understandable grief for the destruction of the opera houses he so treasured—Munich, Dresden, Vienna, Weimar, Berlin—and, beyond that, the great German musical culture that had bred him.[72] Strauss himself referred in his private diaries to "the twelve-year reign of bestiality, ignorance, and anti-culture under the greatest of criminals, during which Germany's two thousand years of cultural evolution met its doom."[73] Yet many continued to believe that *Metamorphosen* was either an apologia for Strauss's initial involvement with (and complacency about) the regime or a confession, an atonement for "guilt and responsibility."[74] Not surprisingly in this situation, the aging and ailing Strauss's depression continued.

Just as Boito tempted Verdi into *Falstaff* by offering him something different in his old age, so Clemens Krauss tried (but failed) to engage Strauss in a project to write an oratorio on Noah's flood: "Now that you are slowly approaching Noah's age the analogy lies near: you too have made an Ark with your music, in which we can save all the good spirits of our art from the flood of atonality."[75] Echoing Verdi's fear of the Germanic flood of Wagnerism in his time, this modernist "flood of atonality" has been seen as yet another factor in Strauss's depression, concerned as he was about both his own musical reputation and "the future of German music in the light of the quickening advance of non-tonal aesthetics."[76] Schoenberg, Hindemith, and Ernst Krenek were all, for Strauss, mere "placers of notes."[77] There is no doubt that he would have liked to see atonality banished from his musical world—an attitude he shared, alas, with the National Socialists. As early as 1935 he had drawn up his own list of the ideal opera repertoire, and absent from the list were those that would later be labeled as "degenerate" by the regime. Even at the end of the war, his ideal list would not change.[78]

In an attempt to relieve his depression, Strauss had earlier begun working his way through all the writings of Goethe—for consolation, inspiration, and perhaps escape. Strauss certainly perceived Goethean parallels with his own life course, writing to a friend: "I am quietly working away for myself (following Goethe's sublime example)."[79] Strauss felt that both he and Goethe had been hardworking artists and lonely protectors of the German tradition.[80] Both had lived long and active lives in ages filled with new ideas. And both went from being revolutionaries to being seen as reactionaries, while just carrying on "in their own fashion."[81] A few years later Strauss would quote to Willi Schuh a letter Goethe had written just a few days before his death: "Confusing conclusions about confusing deeds dominate the world, and I have nothing more pressing to do than if possible to increase that which remains and is left to me and to keep my originality in hand."[82] Strauss's personal interest in this assertion implies much about his response to his historical times and to his own creativity in his older age.

But not even reading Goethe could relieve his depression as he awaited the decision of the denazification tribunal. He desperately needed to get back to work to distract himself from what a friend called his "end-of-the-world mood."[83] His son Franz suggested that he write some songs. This made sense, since Strauss had written songs throughout his composing life. Having earlier read the poem "Im Abendrot," by Joseph von Eichendorff, he felt it had special meaning for him and so set it to music. Then, finally, in June 1948, just before Strauss's eighty-fourth birthday, came the eight-page denazification document that cleared the composer of any incrimination, stating: "He rejected any form of racist policies in art and therefore distanced himself increasingly from influential members of the party who sought to influence art in the sense of Nazi ideology." It also cited the once damning SS report to the Ministry of Propaganda: "It is well known of Strauss that even in the year 1935 he avoided the German greeting in public and had contacts with Jewish circles at home and abroad."[84]

STRAUSS'S *FOUR LAST SONGS*

Upon this announcement, a relieved Strauss returned to the idea of writing more songs. He had been given a copy of the poems of Hermann Hesse the year before, and proceeded to set three of them: "Frühling," "September," and "Beim Schlafengehen."[85] It was not until after his death that these four songs would be grouped together by Ernst Roth, chief editor of the publishing house of Boosey & Hawkes, and given the title of *Four Last Songs*. All four are written for soprano voice and orchestra, with prominent horn parts—again markers of Strauss's musical life review in their clear references to his wife, the soprano Pauline de Ahne, and his father, Franz, the principal horn of the Munich Court Orchestra for almost fifty years.

Whatever date is given to the start of Strauss's Indian summer, everyone agrees that these four orchestral songs are its culmination. Even his harshest critics see in them "renewed creative freshness" and "a resurgence of Strauss's talent"[86]—a talent that, arguably, had always been there. We would argue further that these songs are also the culmination of his musical life review. Again, citation—of himself, set within his beloved German tradition—is one of his major means of signaling the review. For example, in "Beim Schlafengehen," he quotes the Adagio from Beethoven's String Quartet op. 59 no. 1; even more poignant, however, is the rapt violin solo, reminiscent of both *Rosenkavalier* and *Ariadne auf Naxos*, but in fact a direct citation from Strauss's own first opera, *Guntram*.[87] In "Im Abendrot" he echoes, sixty years later, a motif from *Tod und Verklärung* (*Death and Transfiguration*) on the horn, as the soprano sings the word "Tod" (death). And, tellingly, the earlier work's echo feels stylistically appropriate in this latest of works too, precisely because Strauss's style shows so much continuity over the decades.[88]

The words of these chosen songs are significant in themselves for what they suggest about Strauss's state of mind at the time. Though the text concerns the arrival of spring, even "Frühling" opens "in dämmrigen Grüften" (in shadowy crypts),[89] matching the "brooding, dark tonal organization" of the piece, which is strangely autumnal.[90] But with "September" begins a series of images of fatigue, age, and death—of seasons, of the day, of lives. The song ends with summer slowly closing its weary eyes: "Langsam tut er die müdgewordnen Augen zu."[91] "Beim Schlafengehen"

("On Going to Sleep") welcomes night and a deathlike sleep that allows the unfettered soul to soar freely ("die Seele unbewacht will in freien Flügen schweben").[92] And, most movingly, in "Im Abendrot" a weary couple, after a life of "Not und Freude" (sorrow and joy),[93] seeks rest from wandering. Images of sunset and sleep signal "weiter, stiller Friede" (vast, tranquil peace),[94] as the final line questions: "Ist dies etwa der Tod?" (Is this perhaps death?).[95] Changing the poet's original "das" to "dies"—"that" to "this"—Strauss makes the immediacy of the end more powerful and personal. What has been called the music's "rich nostalgic mellifluousness" contributes to that personal impact.[96]

In other words, the poems suggest an acceptance of age and death that has been taken as a sign of the lifting of the composer's depression. Whether the writing of the songs was in itself therapeutic, or whether their thematic resonance of fatigue and dying helped him to accept his fate, is ultimately unknowable—despite the many confident, if also sentimental, assertions that he clearly identified with the emotions expressed in the pieces. While the songs do reveal a certain serene "resignation to the inescapable,"[97] they also mark the completion of Strauss's musical life review. One of his biographers, Michael Kennedy, sees in these songs a "reaffirmation of the glories of tonality, a demonstration of how much new music could still be found in the traditional diatonic and chromatic styles."[98] Less kindly, perhaps, others have seen them, with their soaring melodies, as "the last representatives of [the] nineteenth-century German Romantic Orchestral Lied"—although written in 1948.[99] Either way, the songs have been interpreted by all as movingly autobiographical, as a personal testament to his life—and, we would add, specifically to his life in music. Strauss may still have been Strauss, but he saved some of his best for last.[100] That these songs became canonical in the classical repertoire after Strauss's death is testimony to the enduring power and popularity of his music even through the rise (and fall) of Schoenbergian modernism: audiences always responded positively to the lushness and emotional directness of Strauss's music in a way that they never did to the astringency and intellectual hermeticism of that particular kind of modernism.

The integration that his life review allowed was musical, but for Strauss, music was a large part of his identity. The appropriately named biographical film *Ein Leben für die Musik* (*A Life for Music*), made in the last summer of his life, shows a sturdy-looking eighty-five-year-old Strauss at the piano playing the transformation music from *Daphne* (1937)—perhaps a final message or a desired wish for an easeful end. Before long the failing Strauss would be confined to his bed. He still received friends and shared with them his continuing thoughts about opera's future—and his works' place in it. As he lay on his deathbed, the composer remarked to his daughter-in-law that dying was just as he had imagined it in *Tod und Verklärung*.[101] More than just an anecdote befitting a composer's end, this comment may mark a final step in his life review. Back in 1894, when he was thirty years old, he had described the program of that tone poem in these prescient terms:

> the dying hours of a man who had striven towards the highest ideal-
> istic aims, maybe indeed those of an artist . . . [when] his thoughts
> wander through his past life; his childhood passes before him, the time
> of his youth with its strivings and passions and then, as the pains al-
> ready begin to return, there appears to him the fruit of his life's path,
> the conception, the ideal which he has sought to realize, to present
> artistically, but which he has not been able to complete, since it is not
> for man to be able to accomplish such things. The hour of death ap-
> proaches, the soul leaves the body in order to find gloriously achieved
> in everlasting space those things which could not be fulfilled here
> below.[102]

It was only a week before his death that Strauss would echo these very words in a late conversation with a friend: "There is so much I would still have to do—but I believe that some of what I wanted and have begun has fallen on fertile ground."[103] Strauss's operas are still on the stage today, so he was, in one sense, not wrong—audiences would provide that fertile ground through their happy acceptance of his consistent and highly skilled version of traditional tonal compositional practice. However, for the post-war critics, as we have seen, his compositions would have no place in the modernist world of atonality and serialism. This, however, is the world that Olivier Messiaen would inherit—even if he came to find it sterile. And he would respond with his own idiosyncratic form of late modernism.

CHAPTER FIVE

Olivier Messiaen (1908–1992):
Faith in God and Art

Successful aging entails limiting one's tasks and avoiding excessive demands.
—Robert J. Sternberg and Elena L. Grigorenko,
"Intelligence and Wisdom"

On the evening of Saturday, 21 April 1945, the artistic crème de la crème of Paris met at the Salle du Conservatoire for the premiere of a vocal and instrumental piece called *Trois petites liturgies de la Présence Divine*, whose text and score had both been written by the thirty-six-year-old composer Olivier Messiaen. When it was over the writer Jean Cocteau proclaimed: "There's nothing more to be said after that." "It's Genius," declared the composer Francis Poulenc. Guy Bernard-Delapierre, the director of the Bureau de Concerts de Paris, summed up the positive audience response: "Many musicians, deeply moved, were silent, because the sudden revelation of this masterpiece, in a Paris liberated only a few months earlier and still learning slowly to live again, took on the importance of a great event."[1] But that was not the only response to Messiaen's deliberate attempt to bring his strong Catholic faith into secular spaces. As he himself stated at a later date: "I intended to accomplish a liturgical act, that is to say, to bring a kind of Office, a kind of organized act of praise, into the concert hall."[2] Not everyone was ready for this. Typical of a large segment of the press, Claude Rostand, the critic of *Carrefour*, called it a "work of tinsel, false magnificence and pseudo-mysticism" and infamously compared it to an "angel wearing lipstick."[3] Perhaps religion was not going to sit comfortably or at least not immediately in Parisian concert halls. And, as we shall see, by the time the then seventy-five-year-old composer attempted to ensconce his faith in the opera house with *Saint François d'Assise* (1983), the critical response would be little different—despite his manifest success in the concert hall in the years in between.

THE RELIGIOUS AND THE MUSICAL

Le cas Messiaen (the Messiaen affair), as the subsequent press battle of the mid-1940s came to be known, was provoked by more than this one concert. In the weeks before this premiere Messiaen's radical students from the Paris Conservatoire, led by the ever dismissive young Pierre Boulez, had caused a scandal by scornfully disrupting a concert of works by Igor Stravinsky, one of the reigning musical stars of Paris at the time. The press, arguably, was gunning for Messiaen anyway: here was a successful young composer who had held the prestigious position of organist at the Église de la Sainte-Trinité since he was twenty-two years old, who was writing in a musical style that was not the fashionable one of the day, and who, furthermore, had been publicly critical of Stravinsky's neoclassical works. Messiaen's own musical journalism had shown him to be deeply (and provocatively) engaged in the musical politics of the day.[4] The year before he had had the temerity to publish a book entitled *Technique de mon langage musical* explaining his musical innovations in rhythm and modal composition. And from the start he had always written prefaces, program notes, defenses, and commentaries, and had himself given long talks before performances of his works. In them he explicated at length both their complex technical aspects and their precise religious meaning, for both were equally important to the composer and were intricately connected in his mind. He wanted listeners to experience the divine "beyond" through his music, whose main aim, in his own words, was the "illumination of the theological truths of the Catholic faith."[5] In this, it has been argued, he was consciously living the expected, the appropriate life the church demanded of the religious layperson, engaging (as the catechism puts it) in "temporal affairs and directing them according to God's will."[6]

This unconventional (for the time) religious dimension had driven one irritated critic to complain a few years before: "He seeks to create in his music the power of a personal miracle and then calmly announces that he has succeeded."[7] The Messiaen affair was in fact fought over two related matters. The first was the quality and relevance of those commentaries' mixing of theology and musical theory in what Rostand dismissed as "elaborate gobbledegook."[8] The second was the appropriateness of Messiaen's deliberately sensuous and dynamic sound world to his spiritual topics. In that 1944 treatise he had claimed that the "charm" of the mathematical "impossibilities" in his music's modal and rhythmic domains created a mix of the "voluptuous" and the contemplative that audiences may not, admittedly, understand at first; but the music would "seduce" them anyway and lead them step by step to what he called a "theological rainbow."[9] However one describes it, this was not traditional contemplative religious music, despite titles such as "Le banquet céleste" and "Vingt regards sur l'Enfant-Jésus." This was program music of a sort, because music, for Messiaen, always conveyed meaning; specifically, it communicated the truths of Catholic theology. As Messiaen himself would come to view the terms of this press debate later, "to see someone who was a believer, who had faith . . . and who believed in the Resurrection—they [in the press] couldn't stand it."[10]

FROM SUPERSERIALISM TO BIRDSONG

Deeply hurt by the critics' negative reactions in 1945, Messiaen went uncharacteristically silent: his next works were ostentatiously unaccompanied by commentary. He also turned to less overtly religious topics, specifically, human love—implicitly, however, as a manifestation of divine love. The lush musical palette about which the critics had complained continued in such works as the *Turangalîla-symphonie* (1949) but was considered less provocative on account of the seemingly secular subject matter. Then came a brief but significant period of experimentation. Provoked, perhaps, by his radical students' negative reactions to this music as well as by their own interest in twelve-tone and serial composition, he one-upped even Schoenberg in his *Mode de valeurs et d'intensités* (1949) by "serializing" not only pitch but duration, attack, and intensity. For a brief moment, having become a "superserialist," he was at the center of the musical avantgarde at the famous Darmstadt summer school. In the end, though, he discovered that what he called this "aggressive, intellectual, interesting, gripping" music wasn't sufficiently moving ("émouvant").[11] Unlike many of his intellectualist modernist contemporaries, Messiaen saw emotion as central to music's (in this case theological) impact. Always intellectually and musically curious and open to new ideas,[12] Messiaen also found himself at odds with the "puritanical approach being espoused by the younger generation" of Darmstadt composers, for whom a single kind of serialism (notably, Webern's) was the only acceptable form of modernist "progress."[13] What they prized in Webern's brief and ultracontrolled works was their restricted emotive field, their deliberately limited technical means, and their particular use of preformed elements.[14] The actual preformed elements or preselected compositional materials to which Messiaen turned, in his own idiosyncratic version of this form of modernism, came not from the human imagination, but from God's creation, from what he called, in that early treatise, "nos petits serviteurs de l'immatérielle joie" (our little servants of immaterial joy)[15]—that is, from birds.

An amateur ornithologist from a young age, Messiaen in the 1950s became much more serious, avidly studying birdcalls with respected authorities in France and elsewhere and finding means of transposing or translating them into musical notation. For this deeply religious musician, birds mediated the divine and the human, the spiritual and the physical.[16] But in addition to their symbolic value as messengers of the divine, birds offered a technical confirmation of his own theories of rhythm and improvisation.[17] As one of his biographers, the pianist Peter Hill, put it, this turning to birdsong in his music might well have been his "way of bringing into his music the concerns of the avant garde—the open-ended musical forms, the fluid structuring of time . . . , and, above all, the incorporating into music of 'non-musical' sources of sound."[18]

Indeed, it has been suggested that Messiaen was in fact at an impasse at this point in his composing life, and, as he himself expressed his position a few years later, "In the face of so many opposed schools, of outmoded styles, of contradictory languages, there is no human music capable of restoring confidence to the despairing one. It is at this point that the voices of Nature intervene."[19] As Alex Ross, in *The Rest Is Noise*, explains the resulting music, "In keeping with the aesthetic of the Darmstadt generation, his bird music of the fifties had an impeccably fragmented and pointillistic sound, as if the Cetti's warbler, the blue tit, and the great spotted woodpecker had propounded serialism in advance of Babbitt and Boulez."[20] This was Messiaen's own strange version of modernist music. He would even come to see his use of percussion in the birdsong compositions as directly related to contemporary electronic music or *musique concrète*.[21]

Over the next decades Messiaen's works came to be oriented mainly around the song of birds, which he thought of as the greatest musicians on our planet.[22] His teacher, Paul Dukas, had told him years before, "Ecoutez les oiseaux, ce sont de grands maîtres" (Listen to the birds, they are great masters).[23] And listen he did, carefully, and learn. His first extended birdsong piece, *Réveil des oiseaux* (1953), has been called an important work that "fundamentally reinvented the notion of what constituted a piece of orchestral music."[24] In fact, Boulez would later claim that in it Messiaen "has taught us to look around us and to understand that all can become music."[25] The composer himself was somewhat more self-deprecating and at times almost despairing, lamenting that not only was he a "composer-believer" who speaks of faith to atheists, but an ornithologist speaking "of birds to people who live in cities . . . [who] don't know what birdsongs are."[26]

In time Messiaen returned to overtly religious topics—complete with those familiar explanatory titles and accompanying commentaries on, once again, both the technical and the theological aspects, but adding now the related natural/avian information. When he was approached a few years later to compose a work for the Paris Opéra, he would use the opportunity to bring together and then attempt to surpass all of his musical innovations and place them, as always, in the service of his religious convictions. This, he believed, would be his last and ultimate composition. To set the bar that high, with so much at stake, may well have been hubris: as we shall see, not only did he set himself a daunting theological and musical task, but he also ended up seriously challenging his very sense of self.

THE FIRST (AND LAST) OPERA COMMISSION

That the versatile Messiaen—who composed for organ, piano, orchestra, and voice—would agree to write an opera was not self-evident, however. Although he had studied opera since he was a very young boy—asking for opera scores for Christmas gifts—and had taught opera at the Paris Conservatoire (from Monteverdi to Mozart to Debussy, from Wagner to Berg), he actually thought that the form was now moribund.[27] He felt that after *Wozzeck* (1925) there was no longer any "way forward":[28] "It's impossible in our day to rework the Leitmotif or operas with alternating arias and recitatives; all this, if you [will] excuse me, is out of date. What's to be done then? A new formula must be found; some exist, however: for example, the Japanese Noh and the Balinese theatre."[29] Though the opera he would create, *Saint François d'Assise*, would mark precisely such a "new formula," at first Messiaen didn't feel he had a particular gift for this dramatic musical form. And, after all, he noted, there were only about "ten indisputable masterpieces" anyway.[30] What could he add? Nevertheless, at the age of sixty-seven he signed a contract and began working on an eight-year operatic project that would prove to be a massive and draining undertaking, one requiring multiple postponements of deadlines. It clearly taxed him—creatively, physically, psychologically, and emotionally.

This immense stress was engendered in part because his approach to the creation of his first and last monumental opera was modeled on Wagner's, for Messiaen too was creating a *Gesamtkunstwerk*:[31] he too wanted to do everything himself—the libretto, score, dramaturgy, costumes, sets, lighting, and even casting and placement of the orchestra members in the hall. As might be suspected already from his press-irritating commentaries, Messiaen needed to be in control of the meaning of his works. He later told his frequent interviewer, Claude Samuel, that when he began the opera he already felt like an old man, but he needed to complete this final work before he died in order not to have to depend on others, "postmortem," to finish—or explain—the opera.[32] Since, from the start, he saw this as his last work, he put every ounce of his energy into it.[33]

The question is: why would he choose St. Francis of Assisi for the subject matter of his only opera? In a genre obsessed with the darker passions and driven by dramatic intensity, the life of the gentle thirteenth-century saint was an unlikely topic, especially when Messiaen as librettist carefully pared down to a minimum all the possible episodes of biographical conflict—or, as he wryly put it, "I left out sin."[34] As Daniel Mendelsohn has remarked, however, "Good people do not, generally speaking, make good subjects for opera,"[35] especially saints. But during Messiaen's early years in the 1920s when he was a student at the Paris Conservatoire, no fewer than eight important works on saints, two on Francis himself, were premiered in Paris—all reflecting the "renouveau catholique" of the earlier years of the new century.[36] Before that, in 1912, Gabriel Pierné had composed an oratorio, *Les fioretti de Saint François d'Assise*, and in the late 1930s Charles Tournemire had written *Il poverello di Assisi*. Clearly, somehow this saint was in the Parisian air. Messiaen said that initially he really wanted to write a Passion or a Resurrection but did not feel personally "worthy of it"; he also feared Christ was not or should not be "presentable" on stage.[37] So he chose instead a man, not a god, but the one who resembled Christ the most: he was poor, chaste, humble, but he suffered— and in his stigmata, he suffered Christ's own wounds. For the first time on the operatic stage, audiences would witness what the composer called "the progress of grace in the soul of a saint."[38]

Although Messiaen vehemently denied any autobiographical connection to his saintly subject, he clearly did identify in many complex ways with St. Francis. He remarked to the premiere's assistant conductor, Kent Nagano, that he felt there was a certain parallel in their lives, and to Samuel that he considered the saint a "colleague."[39] He thought of himself as "Franciscan" in his love of nature as the work of God, and of course, while the saint famously preached to the birds, birds in a very real sense spoke to Messiaen. It has been argued that the saint and the composer traveled the same spiritual path in the opera, suggesting that mystic inspiration and aesthetic inspiration ran in parallel.[40] The Angel articulates this linkage to St. Francis in the opera: "Tu parles à Dieu en musique: il va te répondre en musique" (You speak to God in music; He will respond to you in music).[41] Some have argued, not unconvincingly, that this may describe more accurately Messiaen's own relationship to art than that of St. Francis.[42] Certainly the composer always felt that music, the most "immaterial" of the arts, was the one that could allow the best access to the invisible, and thus it was the best equipped to express religious truths.[43] At the end of the opera, the saint sings: "Seigneur! Musique et Poésie m'ont conduit vers Toi" (Lord! Music and Poetry have led me to You),[44] and most critics have heard in these words Messiaen's own testament of faith in both his God and his art.

AGING AND SUFFERING

The particular version of the St. Francis story that Messiaen chose—one that focuses on the saint's suffering—made for not only a nontraditional operatic subject, but also an odd focus even for this religious composer. His works—from his early *Quatuor pour la fin du temps* (1940–41) to the oratorio, *La transfiguration de Notre-Seigneur Jésus-Christ* (1965–69)—were musically and thematically affirmative. Despite having endured the long and painful disintegration of the physical and mental health of his first wife, the violinist Claire Delbos, this was a man whose basic worldview was about as far from modernist angst as could be imagined—the exact opposite of Thomas Mann's famously tortured composer, Adrian Leverkühn, in *Doktor Faustus*.[45] His second marriage, after Delbos's death, to his brilliant former student, the pianist Yvonne Loriod, reinforced his confidence and faith. All his life Messiaen had resolutely and self-consciously expressed a kind of theology of joy, salvation, and glory, ignoring all kinds of negativity, from sin to evil. He used his "musical language as praise—a sense of sacred joy permeating all his work."[46] Here, for the first time, in a massive work that he considered (both at the time and later) the "sum" of all he had done thus far, both technically and religiously,[47] he chose to tell the story not only of the blessed man who preached to the birds, but of the same man who suffered horribly, who offered himself up to both unimaginable physical and psychological pain, in order to find "perfect joy." In Messiaen's own words, the opera "est une oeuvre de lumière, c'est aussi une oeuvre de douleur. Les deux états sont intimement mêlés" (is a work of light, it is also a work of suffering. The two states are intimately mixed together).[48] This was the first depiction of or reference to suffering in his entire oeuvre. Arguably, personal awareness of human frailty and mortality was unavoidable for Messiaen when he began to conceive the opera: Loriod's mother had just died, as had a student and a former teacher; these sudden deaths were quickly followed by those of a close aunt and yet another younger student. At this point, provoked by these painful reminders of mortality, Messiaen tellingly purchased two burial plots. The further deaths of two close musician colleagues, Darius Milhaud and André Jolivet, and another aunt who had helped raise him also haunted the composer in his late years.

It is also perhaps no accident that the aging artist was himself facing physical and psychic suffering in the years of the opera's composition. Apart from one difficult time when he was "dogged by ill-health" in his late forties,[49] when his first wife was so ill and his responsibilities for his young son were so distractingly oppressive, the composer had always been healthy. Now, in his late sixties, things changed radically. He suffered from viral hepatitis and gallstones, and he also had a serious fall, injuring his ankle and face; complications from this necessitated an operation, and he suffered from leg ulcers for the rest of his life. While on the road for his seventieth-birthday celebrations, he suffered a urinary tract obstruction and was hospitalized and operated upon. He had continuing eye problems and began to show early signs of arthritis in his right hand. In the midst of all this he had also been forced to retire from the Conservatoire at age seventy, after almost forty years of teaching, thereby losing an important social and professional role.

Then came the moment of crisis: in 1981, when he had fallen badly behind schedule in orchestrating the opera, he developed a new set of symptoms: a sore throat, an inability to sleep, an irregular heartbeat. Not surprisingly, perhaps, these marked an emotional as well as physical crisis: remember what was at stake for Messiaen here. If one's entire sense of personhood is based, as it was in this case, upon the desire to create a work that is the musical apotheosis of one's religious beliefs, what happens if one has worries about the possibility of failure? As Loriod recalled, "Messiaen was subdued and exhausted, unable to decide what to do; he was prone to fits of weeping, and was convinced the opera would never be finished."[50] But finished it eventually was. Nagano, who worked with the composer as the work came to the stage, revealingly wrote:

> Messiaen told me that his life's work was finished—"I've lived to write *Saint François* and I feel that I'm not going to write any more"—and he said this in such a way that I felt he was referring to the end of his

life. . . . [Messiaen said:] "I feel something is happening. I tell you, Kent, if I live long enough to hear the first orchestral rehearsal I'll be happy." Then after the first rehearsal Messiaen said, "I just wish I could see a rehearsal on stage." So we got into the opera house and did the first rehearsal on stage, but Messiaen said, "You know if I could hear just one complete run-through of my opera then I'd know it's been created." We had the dress rehearsals, and then the first performance, and Messiaen not only survived but by the end was in remarkably good health.[51]

Yet, the composer really had been extended to the limit of his resources—all his resources—in finishing this opera about death and suffering as the means to resurrection and joy.

THE TRIALS OF (AND IN) *SAINT FRANÇOIS D'ASSISE*

With over four hours of music (over five hours in performance), *Saint François d'Assise* is a massive work. As Messiaen stated, "Having reached the end of my career, I had all the same a right to take my time expressing myself."[52] He rightly pointed out that Wagner's operas (which he had taught and appreciated for years) are long too, adding: "I don't see why one wouldn't write a long work if the subject warrants it." Indeed, many have seen the orchestral magnitude, the musical scope, and the religious inspiration of *Saint François* as a direct response to Wagner's own last opera, *Parsifal*. Messiaen's decidedly long score, in eight volumes, weighs over twenty kilograms. It calls for 119 orchestral players and 150 singers in the chorus (though this, in fact, represents a reduction in his initial conception of musical forces). Seiji Ozawa, the conductor of the premiere, is said by the composer himself, upon first seeing the score, to have called it "madness".[53] There are seven soloists, two of them forming the centerpieces: St. Francis, a baritone, who is on stage for most of the opera, and the Angel, a soprano and the only female voice heard. Each of the soloists, however, is given at least one unique musical theme and a characteristic birdsong. The sung parts, in their accentuated declamation, resemble medieval psalmody, written in a barer, sparer style than was usual for Messiaen. The reason he gave for this simplicity was theological: the words must be heard; the Christian message was important. In stark contrast with this ascetic vocalization, the orchestral sound palette is extraordinarily rich and differentiated.[54] This aural opposition may well reflect, as it has been suggested, the Franciscan ideal of humankind's self-restriction versus the splendor of God.[55]

The libretto was constructed by Messiaen himself of quotations taken from many sources: early biographies of the saint; the anonymous medieval works known as the *Fioretti* and the *Considerations on the Holy Stigmata*; St. Francis's own writings; the Scriptures; Thomas à Kempis's *Imitation of Christ*; and the writings of St. Thomas Aquinas. From the start he had always preferred to write his own lyrics, he said, because of his music's "great rhythmic complexity" and thus the need to adapt the words to his rhythms.[56] The language used is not complexly metaphorical, as in some of his earlier song cycles such as *Poèmes pour Mi* (1937) or *Chants de terre et de ciel* (1938), but instead is simple and intended to be easily understood. The action, such as it is, takes place in eight relatively static tableaux, divided into three acts. In performance, then, this is far from a typical opera. Messiaen himself called it a "musical spectacle,"[57] and others have made convincing links to oratorio, to the medieval miracle or mystery play, and even to the Catholic Stations of the Cross. The composer talked specifically about the influence of the slowness and stylization of Japanese Noh theater, some of which also deals with the supernatural world, of course. In the opera he drew upon Noh conventions explicitly when presenting the Angel, in the expressionistic character of the music and the desired, very slow mode of moving (as if on air).[58]

This story of suffering begins with Brother Leo expressing a strong fear of death to Francis: "J'ai peur, j'ai peur sur la route" (I am afraid, I am afraid on the road),[59] he repeats here and throughout the opera. The subsequent three images he deploys make clear that this road is the road of life, leading to death: the Franciscan friar fears the moment, he explains, when the windows (eyes) grow large and more obscure, when the leaves of the poinsettia no longer turn red, and when the gardenia is no longer perfumed. In response Francis endeavors to teach him the paradoxical meaning of the "perfect joy" achieved only through pain, suffering, and rejection, all borne patiently and willingly, even cheerfully, as Christ did in His passion and death on the cross. At the end of the next tableau Francis is heard praying to the God of beauty who, he has come to realize, has also allowed ugliness to exist in the world. He admits his specific loathing of lepers, with their ravaged faces and their stale and horrible stench, and therefore prays that God make him capable of loving a leper. In the third scene's staging of pain as well as ugliness, Francis is confronted with the horrific physical and psychological suffering of a man with a body covered with pustules, whose itching and pain torment him greatly, and who is avoided by all, even those who seek to help him. He even disgusts himself, he says. Rejecting with vehemence the conventional religious consolations offered by Francis, the Leper is only brought to accept his fate by an Angel—whom the audience sees, but whom the stage characters only hear. Francis then kisses the Leper, and two miracles simultaneously occur: the Leper is cured and Francis becomes St. Francis.

Act 2 opens with a reminder of Brother Leo's fear of death once again, but the central focus is on the arrival of a mysterious traveler at the monastery, introduced by a supernaturally loud knocking at the door. It soon becomes clear to the audience, if not the Franciscans, that this is the same Angel whom we have just heard and seen and who, in the next tableau, will speak directly to the saint about the power of music and then play for him the ineffable "musique de l'invisible."[60] This leaves St. Francis in an unconscious swoon, in his words, "terrassé, anéanti par . ... cette musique céleste" (laid low, overwhelmed by . . . this celestial music).[61] What we have just heard, along with him, are the strange sounds of three ondes martenot, electronic instruments whose eerie tones and high register the composer often used to evoke the otherness of the heavenly.[62] If attempting to orchestrate the divine was a difficult enough task for a composer, it turned out to be nothing, in his own mind, compared to what Messiaen tackled in the next tableau, the Sermon to the Birds. The composer wanted this to be the best birdsong music he had ever written, and to that end he used the songs of over forty different birds from all over the world in this long, forty-five-minute section.

For over thirty years Messiaen had been transcribing birdsong on his travels, though "transcribing" does not capture the complexity of the process that Peter Hill rightly calls "creative reconstruction."[63] Each note of a bird's song had to be given a chord, a complex of sounds that would translate the timbre of the note. (For a long piece, therefore, this meant inventing up to two thousand harmonies.) Because birds are smaller and their hearts beat faster, their songs' tempi and rhythms also had to be transposed to human time and their pitches lowered for human instruments. Messiaen then had to suppress the songs' tiny intervals that our instruments could not execute, while respecting the scale of values of the different intervals.[64] This was difficult enough to do; but to then move to orchestrate all of these birdsongs together was a gargantuan task, one he left to the very end of the compositional process. Orchestrating especially the concert of the birds, the avian response to the saint's preaching, left Messiaen physically exhausted. The actual writing out of the entire opera had been a real challenge to a composer in his seventies, as he once explained to the man who had commissioned it, Rolf Liebermann: "I had to write on sheets with 72 staves; thus I could only work standing. The huge sheets were spread out across the table, with me standing before it, the double bass in my stomach and the piccolo at the other side of the table. Half lying on the table, for years; I was literally finished."[65] If this section of the opera was a challenge for the composer to orchestrate, it would prove equally difficult for the conductor, who has to maintain a precise beat for one part of the orchestra while at the same time signaling when each of the birdsongs should enter, then allowing them to play at their own tempo independently of the rest of the orchestra.[66] The great polytempo "organized disorder" that is then heard (and that Messiaen said he learned from the birds themselves) was assessed by its creator: "Even if it is madness, the result is marvelous! I was looking for and achieved a great, organized chaos of which I know no equivalent in contemporary music."[67]

While this was the scene that Messiaen cared most about, the one closest to his heart, it was the next one that caused him the most imaginative difficulty, for it went most against his musical and religious personality: the scene of the painful inflicting of Christ's stigmata upon the body of St. Francis. What the composer evocatively called the "orchestre d'angoisse" (orchestra of anguish) creates a nightmarish aural world of "savage harmonies and unheard-of sound effects";[68] interestingly, this is the only part of the opera in which Messiaen uses serial techniques. In his own words, perhaps thinking back to his early and now abandoned experiment, "this super-serial passage gives you an idea of my feelings about serial music: I find it capable of expressing only fear, terror, and night."[69] In this scene the chorus takes on the voice of Christ as we listen and watch what the saint deems his "unworthy body" taking upon itself the physical suffering of the Son of God and then experiencing the love which allows the acceptance of that extreme pain.

TRANSCENDENCE AND "DAZZLEMENT"

Messiaen said he could not end the opera with the death of St. Francis: "for me, as a believer, death is only the passing to a new life in eternity."[70] For this reason, the final tableau is called "Death and the New Life." Saying farewell to the other Franciscans, the saint welcomes "notre soeur la Mort corporelle, la Mort! à qui nul homme ne peut échapper" (our sister, bodily Death, Death! from whom no man can escape).[71] In his final words, St. Francis acknowledges, as noted earlier, that music and poetry had led him (as they had Messiaen) to God, and begs the Lord, in his words, "illumine-moi de ta Présence! Délivre-moi, enivre-moi, éblouis-moi pour toujours de ton excès de Vérité" (illumine me with Your Presence! Deliver

me, enrapture me, dazzle me forever by Your excess of truth).[72] Trans-
ported, he dies into a new life as the chorus underlines the final message:
"de la douleur, de la faiblesse, et de l'ignominie: il ressuscite de la Force,
de la Gloire, de la Joie!!!" (from suffering, from weakness, from ignominy:
He resuscitates the Power, the Glory, the Joy!!!).[73] The music that accompanies the move into eternity is a startling and affirmative C major chord—
traditional, perhaps, yet one usually shunned by his contemporaries.[74] This
triumphant and simple music contrasts with the rich harmonic spectrum
of the rest of the piece, with its wide range of opulent colors and expressive values. Associated in the composer's mind (as in many others') with
light, this resplendent major chord signals transcendent light, the musical
dazzlement or *éblouissement* that Messiaen wanted and expected his audience to experience.

Éblouissement came to be a key word in the composer's thinking: he
felt that the sensual and emotional effect of his music should be like that
of the spiritual suspension of the barriers of perception after death—an
experience, in other words, of transcendence.[75] Throughout his composing
life, all of his experiments in rhythm, especially his "non-retrogradable
rhythms" that "reproduce themselves in reverse,"[76] had been aimed at
expressing a new form of temporality: that of the eternal experienced in
time.[77] Likewise, on the harmonic level, his experiments in "modes of
limited transposition" offered the same kind of internal symmetries, for
they are scales that reproduce themselves on transposition. Such symmetries were, for Messiaen, musical symbols of immutability—that is, of
eternity, the time of God. In a resolutely linear medium, music, he sought
to suspend that linear, causal, progress-oriented time; he wanted to juxta-
pose and contrast sounds vertically, statically, with no beginning, middle,
or end, rather than have the music proceed in the traditional narrative or
horizontal fashion. Refusing the customary Western transitions and harmonic resolutions, this music was to have no European "time sense";[78]
it was to move beyond rational understanding. *Éblouissement* would in
this way bring about what he called "a breakthrough toward the beyond"
through specifically *aesthetic* dazzlement, through *music*.[79]

The textual citations and repetitions with variations in the libretto
text, it has been argued, were intended to work in the same way: making
present moments of the past, changing thereby our perception of time.[80]
Similarly, the opera's quasi-ritual, static stylizations, its slow tempi, its
expansive sound planes were all meant to create a sense of time expanded,
even standing still: the timeless in the temporal.[81] Even Messiaen's particular form of synesthesia—the intellectual (not, in his case, neurological)

linking of colors to sounds—became part of this effect of *éblouissement*: in his words, music like his own, music that was "colored," "[touche] à la fois nos sens les plus nobles: l'ouïe et la vue, elle ébranle notre sensibilité, excite notre imagination, accroît notre intelligence, nous pousse à dépasser les concepts, à aborder ce qui est plus haut que le raisonnement et l'intuition, c'est-à-dire, la Foi" (affects both of our most noble senses: hearing and sight, it shakes up our sensibility, excites our imagination, increases our intelligence, pushes us to go beyond concepts, to approach that which is higher than reasoning and intuition, that is, Faith).[82]

In other words, this was not meant to be, nor was it, an opera meant simply to entertain a public. It was intended to be something totally new in form and content on the operatic stage, but at the same time, it was to be familiar—recalling the rituals of the church and other dramatic forms (Stations of the Cross, miracle plays, oratorio). Ross memorably calls the opera "a village mystery play on a Wagnerian scale."[83] In this sense it was consciously both a summation of its composer's entire being—musical and theological[84]—and an innovation, for, as he himself put it, "any original work inevitably breaks with certain traditions,"[85] in this case, operatic traditions. In subsequent years the critics would agree with him that the massive work was a *summa*, while also concurring that there was progression as well. Despite the obvious changes in genre, length, subject matter, and sheer complexity, they noted many continuities with his earlier works on various levels, making this a kind of grand summation of his musical language: harmonic procedures and motifs reappeared;[86] the birdsong never went away after the 1950s, of course; and the early electronic instrument Messiaen favored, the ondes martenot, came into play once again, as did writing for the voice. Like Wagner's *Ring* and Debussy's *Pelléas et Mélisande*—both influential works for *Saint François*—there is here a rich network of symbolic cross-references to earlier works.[87] And, of course, Messiaen's Christian inspiration never faltered. For many later critics, the opera was the grand and successful conclusion not only to eight years of labor, but also to an entire spiritual and artistic lifetime of work.[88]

LATE STYLE: RECEPTION—AND AFTERMATH

When the opera finally premiered on 28 November 1983 at the Palais Garnier in Paris, many contemporaries agreed. This was "du Messiaen tout pur" (pure Messiaen), according to Jacques Longchamp in *Le monde*, but it was more "humanized" and richer than anything that had preceded it.[89] The work was greeted with "ferveur et admiration," according to the reviewer from *Le Figaro*, who also cited Cardinal Lustiger as having enjoyed the provocation of seeing this sacred subject matter treated in what he saw as a place of luxury, illusion, and sensuality.[90] Another reviewer proclaimed it "un puissant . . . un écrasant chef-d'oeuvre" (a powerful . . . an overwhelming masterpiece).[91] But it was left to Sylvie de Nussac at *L'express* to declare it "l'aboutissement, peut-être l'apothéose, de l'oeuvre et du langage tout à fait singulier de Messiaen" (the successful completion, perhaps the apotheosis, of the totally singular work and language of Messiaen).[92]

Yet, as the composer himself admitted, while some of the reviews were decidedly laudatory, others were not.[93] Predictably, some audience members simply didn't like their opera "contaminated" by religion, but preferred to be entertained.[94] The continuities with Messiaen's earlier work, treasured by both later critics and some contemporary reviewers, were seen by others at the time as self-plagiarism: what were once innovations were now seen only as "tics, ressassements, obsessions rythmiques, manie harmonique, idées fixes orchestrales" (tics, rehashings, rhythmic obsessions, old harmonic habits, orchestral *idées fixes*).[95] In the *Nouvel observateur* the opera was criticized for its absence of dramatic inspiration;[96] in *Libération* it was attacked for its static quality and its "painful" Hollywood lighting effects (making visible onstage the colors the composer perceived in the music)—all blamed on Messiaen's overly tight control over the production.[97] There may have been some truth to this, for, it must be admitted, he did have immense influence on the production. And he also had little practical experience of opera as a live theatrical form: to him, opera was more a text to be studied.

Messiaen himself felt that some of these attacks were as malicious as those against the *Trois petites liturgies* in 1945, though worded "in more respectable turns-of-phrase."[98] He speculated that this was because he was older and people knew he had also devoted eight years of work to the piece. One of the strongest of these attacks, however, was a telling one: "Pourquoi ce jeu liturgico-mystique, si ce n'est pour donner satisfaction aux fantasmes religieux d'un homme âgé qui fut pourtant, en son temps, un créateur d'avant-garde?" (Why this liturgicomystical game, if not to satisfy the religious fantasies of an old man who was, however, in his day an avant-garde creator?).[99] To recall Messiaen's advancing age and avant-garde past may have been an insult, but it was a subject on the composer's mind as well. Just before opening night he told an interviewer who asked what he would do next: "Rien, c'est comme un grand temps blanc" (Nothing, it's like a great blank time).[100] The elation he understandably felt at the premiere inevitably dissipated. He went from an initial sense of completion—he is cited in *Libération* the day after the opening as saying, "Twilight has arrived. I have finished. I will never compose anything else"[101]—to a feeling of emptiness: physically and emotionally exhausted, he had put everything of himself into the opera and now felt "fini comme compositeur" (finished as a composer).[102]

Later on Messiaen would interpret this in two different ways. In 1989 he said he really thought his career was finished at that time and became depressed over the fact that he had nothing left to say.[103] But even later, in 1992, just before his death, he put it more positively: he thought he had said everything he had to say in the opera and that therefore he *could* now stop composing, because his work was completed ("je pensais avoir tout dit, que je pouvais m'arrêter de composer").[104] But there is no doubt that for this deeply Catholic composer, who had dedicated his life and his work to expressing the truths of his faith, not to write music again would constitute a significant threat to his very sense of personhood. Those last words he gave to St. Francis articulate his personal belief that poetry and music had brought him to God. Not to be an active composer was to cut himself off from this sense of his self, especially in relation to his faith.

Nevertheless, this bout of aesthetic postpartum depression turned out to be relatively short-lived, for within a year he began composing his most extensive work for what was, for him, a purely religious instrument, the organ—indeed, for the one that he played at the Église de la Sainte-Trinité every week. *Livre du Saint Sacrement* was based on those weekly improvisations, further inspired by a trip to Israel, where he saw the sites of the Bible and Christ's life.[105] But travel, success, and age began to take their physical and psychological toll: Messiaen and Loriod were in the habit of attending performances of his work all over the world, and the now "establishment" artist began to receive multiple awards and honors—all of which made their own attendant demands on his time and energy. But it turned out to be a commission by his former student, the radical composer and conductor Pierre Boulez, for a modest orchestral piece in 1984 that would prove to be another kind of breaking point for the aging composer. Unable to make repeatedly postponed deadlines, the exhausted Messiaen came "close to despair," losing all self-confidence and self-belief.[106]

Why? The composer was notoriously private, indeed secretive, about his personal life. While expounding publicly at great length in order to guide and control the meaning of his compositions, he paradoxically said and wrote so very little about his inner states or his creative processes that Claude Samuel dubbed him "Messiaen, homme du secret" (man of secrets).[107] Therefore we are left to interpret and speculate. Could it be that having to write a new and different piece for Boulez, his most critical and, in his eyes, his most brilliant former student—a piece that implicitly would need to demonstrate the "progress" of Messiaen's own particular version of modernism—turned out to be too reminiscent of the earlier difficulty in completing the opera, but now in secular (musical) terms? Again, physical suffering, this time from back pain and arthritis, likely made his situation even more difficult. During these years, however, he did manage to write a small set of pieces for piano called *Petites esquisses d'oiseaux*. While Loriod found in these "a new kind of pianism, 'poetic and sublime'" because of their unaccustomed spareness (a description that recalls the familiar truisms of late-style discourse), the composer himself was more negative, claiming, "I'm tired, I can no longer write, the pieces are not very good."[108] After trying unsuccessfully to extricate himself from the Boulez commission, Messiaen slowly regained his confidence over the next few years, finally completing the eight-minute, long-promised piece, *Un vitrail et des oiseaux*, and even accepting an extensive new commission from Zubin Mehta for the New York Philharmonic's 150th anniversary. This, *Éclairs sur l'au-delà . . .* , would be considered his last major work and would only be performed after his death. Before he could complete it, his health began to fail once again: he experienced blackouts and, as a result, serious falls. His mobility therefore decreased, but he continued to travel to performances of his works, even though he was forced to use a wheelchair in airports.

Interestingly, those contradictory evaluations of Messiaen's late style that emerged in response to *Saint François* made a reappearance in almost exactly the same terms with *Éclairs*. For some, this vast orchestral piece marked the "crowning of a lifetime's obsession with the nuances of timbre,"[109] as well as with Mozartian melodic lines. It was seen as the sum of all his themes—birds, love, the cosmos, divine glory, apocalypse, grace, and paradise—as well as of all his musical theories.[110] His musical revisiting of his earlier techniques was seen by some as a continuation, indeed even of a building onward: Messiaen, wrote Paul Griffiths, "was able, in his eighties, to achieve again what he had achieved as a young man, without any dimming, and certainly without any nostalgia."[111] The only signs of age, he went on to say, were positive ones that come from "serene confidence": the work's "orchestral virtuosity, its breadth of reference, and perhaps also its audacity." The negative evaluation of Messiaen's recapitulative impulses was also a now familiar one: that his "music is assembled from a limited set of tried and tested parts, both musical (chords, melodic styles, structures, and so forth) and biographical-referential (the Celestial City, landscapes, stained glass, birds, and the like)."[112] From this perspective, the "semi-automatous," "mechanical" modus operandi produced "reiterative, repeatable" music, almost as predictable as the composer's "rehearsed standard version of his own life story and invariable explanatory notes," according to one critic.[113] What is clear is that, in his biographer's words, "he kept to his course through the artistic upheavals of his time"—however one feels about that consistency.[114]

Indeed, Messiaen continued to compose to the end, and in much the same style. In the last year of his life he wrote a number of short pieces and continued to work assiduously on the enormous theoretical work—the "travail énorme"[115]—he had promised his publisher: the *Traité de rythme, de couleur et d'ornithologie*, whose final assembly Loriod would complete after his death. His health declined rapidly, however, and after palliative surgery for back pain, he died on 27 April 1992. Though he continued to be creative in his last years, *Saint François d'Assise* obviously marked a kind of theological and musical—that is, personal and professional—milestone for Messiaen. It was his greatest challenge; it caused him his greatest anguish. Loriod certainly saw the parallels between the opera's protagonist and its composer: in 1998, she wrote of her late husband's "bonté incroyable, son héroïsme dans les souffrances, les incompréhensions, vraiment il était (comme le disent tous ses amis, ses élèves et ses anciens détracteurs) un génie et un saint" (unbelievable goodness, his heroism in his suffering, [others'] lack of understanding, really he was [as all his friends, students and former detractors say] a genius and a saint).[116] While his bizarre, monumental, late-modernist opera was, in Messiaen's mind, the culmination of his personal religious and musical achievement, returning to composing after it turned out to be crucial to his sense of himself as an artist and as a Christian—that is, as a person. These final works—both theoretical and musical—allowed him to continue the process of fulfilling his life's mission. His musical creativity remained resilient in the face of both the psychological and the physical challenges that age brought with it.

CHAPTER SIX

Benjamin Britten (1913–1976):
The Life Narratives of the
Ever-Young "Working Composer"

Dearest Beth,

Don't worry about me—once this spate of work is over (with luck, before Easter)
I am going off into Hospital so they can find out what really *is* wrong, & I prom-
ise to do exactly what they say. But no one expects anything very serious, or
something that can't be coped with. (Benjamin Britten to Beth Britten Wolford,
12 February 1973, from Aldeburgh)

W riting to his sister as the symptoms of his congestive heart failure
worsened, the fifty-nine-year-old Benjamin Britten had no way of
knowing that he was very wrong about his expectations concerning his
health. Though an active and seemingly healthy man throughout most of
his life, he had had intimations of cardiac problems before this: in February 1968, in his mid-fifties, he had suffered a long bout of what was di-
agnosed as bacterial endocarditis. At that time, what the long hospitalization and extended antibiotic treatment mostly meant to him was an
irritating break in his composing. At first, he called it *"awfully* frustrating" with "only a certain amount of discomfort & pain, & infinite boredom!"[1] However, shortly he would write to his friend William Plomer: "By
breaking all doctors' orders, & really thrashing my poor old self, I have
finished [his "church parable"] Prodigal Son—score and all." But he continued: "My progress is very uneven: some days I feel terrific, & the others low & depressed."[2] This drive to keep composing in difficult medical circumstances and this mixed psychological state would be things
with which Britten would come to be only too familiar over the next
few years.

Shortly after writing that note to his sister, Britten completed his last opera, *Death in Venice*, but it had been very difficult—not in terms of inspiration, but in terms of his health, for he had been experiencing increasingly debilitating symptoms of heart failure. Whether the medical cause of this shortness of breath and weakness was rheumatic heart disease, exacerbated by the bout of endocarditis, or, as Paul Kildea has recently argued, tertiary syphilis, the important fact for our story was that he felt an urgent need to try to relieve those symptoms by undergoing cardiac valve surgery, in the relatively early days of such interventions.[3] The surgery's failure to alleviate the symptoms, combined with a stroke suffered during the operation, led to major changes in his subsequent life. In the few short years between the surgery and his death in 1976 at the age of only sixty-three, Britten was forced to undergo many of the changes we usually associate with aging over a longer period of time: specifically, physical decline, indeed impairment,[4] dependency, and the facing of his imminent demise. It was as if the onset of his physical infirmities marked, in his own eyes and in those of others, his sudden entry into "old old age."

THE PERSISTENCE OF YOUTH

This rapid aging must have been particularly difficult for Britten because, as we shall see, he had always identified with the young and the youthful. He had been athletically active since his school days; indeed, friends found him intensely competitive in tennis and squash as an adult.[5] But there were other factors making the descent into older age stressful for someone who had been a child prodigy: he had begun to compose music at the age of five and played the piano from early on with an ease and skill that would prefigure his subsequent brilliant career as a collaborative pianist.[6] He had been born in Lowestoft, on Britain's east coast, in 1913 and, most auspiciously, on 22 November, the day dedicated to the patron saint of music, St. Cecilia. Encouraged and promoted by his musical mother—to whom he was passionately devoted and who, it was rumored, always planned for him to be the "fourth B" after Bach, Beethoven, and Brahms—he had been both precocious and prolific almost from the start. The British composer Frank Bridge had taken him on as a composition student when he was only in his early teens, and prizes and commissions came his way very quickly, as did opportunities for public performance, both live and on the BBC. His conducting career also began in his teen years, coinciding with the increase in his public performances at the piano and the rapid entry of his compositions into the repertoire. It was likely his disapproval of the "bumbling amateurism" he saw in English music circles at the time that motivated his early desire to be a conductor-composer on the model of Mahler or Strauss before him, as well as a pianist-composer in the earlier romantic mode.[7]

During a stint in the 1930s writing film music for John Grierson's experimental GOP Film Unit, as well as for both Capitol and Strand Films, Britten developed still more new skills—including what the poet W. H. Auden would call his "extraordinary musical sensitivity in relation to the English language," and what others would refer to as his "legendary ability and capacity to solve problems on the spot" involving the interaction of words and music.[8] Throughout his life (except, as we shall see, in certain moments of depression), Britten was blessed with technical fluency and speed, what friend and composer Michael Tippett called his "wonderful facility."[9] But his lifelong work ethic also made Britten believe that everything was really the result of much hard work and considerable technique.[10] What he was most of all, in his own eyes, was a professional working composer. This is one of his two life narratives, one that he had been developing from his early years as his self-defining identity and to which he clung for meaning and support throughout his life, right to the very end.

Though as a young man Britten had been writing incidental music for radio and theater, both in England and then in the United States, his first real piece of musical theater—what he thought of as a high school opera—*Paul Bunyan*, was premiered in 1941 at Columbia University while Britten was living in the United States. Feeling dominated by its librettist, Auden—Britten's friend and life mentor, in a sense—the composer claimed to have learned much from the experience about what *not* to write for the theater.[11] By 1945, when *Peter Grimes* opened the first postwar season of Sadler's Wells Theatre, Britten had arrived as the English opera composer everyone had been waiting for: his music was English, but with an openness to contemporary European music perhaps only matched by that of Frank Bridge.[12] The major operas that followed in quick succession cemented his central role in British operatic life: *The Rape of Lucretia* (1946), *Albert Herring* (1947), *Billy Budd* (1951), *Gloriana* (1953), *The Turn of the Screw* (1954), *A Midsummer Night's Dream* (1960), and *Owen Wingrave* (1971), as well as the equally important children's operas and church parables. But this massive operatic output actually marks only a fragment of his total musical creation over these years. A prolific composer, Britten wrote many song cycles and much instrumental music, usually for particular performers or occasions. Then, as his health declined, he began what he soon came to realize would be his last major opera.

DEATH IN VENICE, ILLNESS IN ALDEBURGH

Sensing that his time was limited, Britten threw himself into composing *Death in Venice*. And like Verdi and Messiaen under similar circumstances, this was a total commitment: creative, physical, and emotional.
He wrote to the choreographer Frederick Ashton that he was "desperately
keen to make it the best thing I have ever done."[13] In the end, he felt it
was "either the best or the worst music I've ever written,"[14] but important
enough to have postponed surgery—at the risk of his life. His partner, the
tenor Peter Pears (for whom he was writing the main part), feared that
the opera was killing him.[15] Ian Tait, Britten's physician throughout these
years, explained that they had an understanding: the composer agreed to
go for tests and surgery as soon as the opera was completed, as indeed he
told his sister he would, if the doctor would agree to try to keep him going with drug therapy until that time.[16] Having also consented to restrict
other activities, he took on no conducting or performing engagements. His
assistants, Colin Matthews and Rosamund Strode, did all they could to
spare his strength for composing; he even agreed to have Steuart Bedford
conduct the opera's premiere, rather than do so himself, as he customar-
ily did. He completed *Death in Venice* but was too ill to attend the opening. Hospitalized shortly after finally seeing a cardiologist, he soon underwent aortic valve replacement surgery, during which he had that ischemic
episode.

   The stroke's compromising of his right hand and leg affected his confidence immensely. Tait felt that the impairment had "very much under-
mined" his will to go on, sensing that the composer "felt drained of creative drive after *Death in Venice* was completed, and was half ready to give
up."[17] Gifted with extraordinary facility and control over the keyboard and
much admired for his pianistic skill, Britten had been an important per-
former, a collaborative pianist who had always accompanied Pears in re-
cital. That part of his creative life was now over: Strode recorded the "abject look of total misery" on his face when he tried to play the piano after
the stroke.[18] As he wrote to his sister Beth, "Of all the things I cannot do
now, the thing I mind about the most is not being able to play the piano."[19]
Though he had never composed at the piano, he always played through his
pieces to exercise "his critical faculties aurally," as Strode noted.[20] Interestingly, he would never again write for the piano: the vocal works written after the surgery were either unaccompanied or accompanied by harp,
harpsichord, or small orchestra. For example, *Canticle V*, op. 89, was scored
for his friend, the celebrated harpist Osian Ellis, and as his biographer Mi-

chael Kennedy has remarked, "Writing for the harp seems to have spurred his imagination to new but economical effects."[21] In fact, Kennedy sees in this work's writing for the voice a "broad but subtle expressiveness" that is characteristic of *Death in Venice*: in other words, he sees continuity, not change, in Britten's technique and style. The harp also replaced the piano in Britten's last song cycle a year later, *A Birthday Hansel*. Like *Canticle V*, it illustrates not only the composer's new physical limitations but also the workings of his innovative imagination.

Britten's letters in the years between the surgery and his death are revealing for what they tell us about the composer's initial crisis of confidence in the face of physical incapacity and his initial depression at the loss of productivity—two serious threats to his creative life narrative as a working composer.[22] Impairment, in this case, involved what Michael Bury calls "biographical disruption" in two different senses.[23] First of all, there was the major reconfiguring of physical identity that occurred when he went from being a lively tennis player to being unable to climb the stairs without becoming short of breath, unable even to compose music normally because his newly impaired right hand wouldn't reach to the top of the page (a problem solved by cutting the long music sheets in half). The second threat was to his creative identity and came in terms of his productivity: Britten's work ethic was legendary, as were his discipline and energy, and he needed to work to feel alive.[24] The first year after the surgery he composed little, writing to Plomer that he was enduring "rather a dreary time with (it seems) more 'downs' than 'ups.'"[25] His sister Barbara tellingly wrote to him a few months after this, saying, "I do wonder how the breathing is getting on & whether you have given up bursting into tears!!"[26]

Depressed, constantly worrying about his new limitations, irritated at being dependent upon others, the composer complained to all his friends and colleagues about his frustration at not being able to get back to work.[27] But, beginning gradually by revisiting earlier pieces and revising them, he slowly returned to composition. He himself admitted later that "for a time after the operation, I couldn't compose because I had no confidence in my powers of selection. I was worried too about my ideas. Then I suddenly got my confidence back and composing has become a marvelous therapy. . . . I have the feeling of being of some use once more."[28] Working, he said, "gets me back on the rails again."[29] From an early age, he had been unhappy if a day went by without composing.[30] This is one of two major life narratives that together might be argued to have given Britten's life coherence and meaning.

Because of this narrative, the relationship between working, being "of some use," and having to conquer depression is one that by this point was familiar to Britten. Throughout his life he had frequent bouts of depression during which he displayed a lack of confidence in his work and often experienced a creative block.[31] Physical health issues would not necessarily stop him from composing, as we saw in the response to his hospitalization with endocarditis, during which he finished *The Prodigal Son*.[32] In fact, it was quite typical of him to compose during a convalescence, even as a boy: it was "almost as though he had been composing feverishly in his head during the period of enforced rest, and could thus write down the resulting music with great speed once he was back at his desk."[33] But what he readily admitted were psychosomatic illnesses often accompanied his depressions, and those (plus overwork) did interfere with his composing: his doctors would periodically treat him for exhaustion by ordering him to take months off.[34] But the combination of debilitating physical impairment and depression after the heart surgery proved to be a difficult, though not insurmountable, hurdle for the man who thought of himself as a working composer.

CREATIVITY VERSUS PRODUCTIVITY

Indeed, it is because he was such a prolific and industrious artist that the relative paucity of postsurgery works stands out: Britten produced nine independent post–*Death in Venice* works in his last years. But these works challenge the postindustrial linking of creativity with productivity that we noted in the first chapter. After all, if an artist can still bring to his creative work the powers of invention, inquiry, openness, spontaneity, formal command—in short, all the things we associate today with creativity— should the quantity of the works produced matter at all?

Britten certainly composed fewer works in his last years, and some would see this as a sign of decline. But when we look at those last works, many see, to use Arnold Whittall's words, "no sudden change of direction, . . . no sudden drying up of his own intensely personal reserves of invention and imagination."[35] It is true that like many aging composers, Verdi, Strauss, and Messiaen among them, Britten looked back in his last works to his earlier compositions. *Death in Venice* has been seen as his musical autobiography with its echoes of *Peter Grimes, Billy Budd, Albert Herring, Curlew River, Gloriana*, and other works.[36] Britten subsequently reworked material from *Death in Venice* in the last movement (revealingly subtitled "La Serenissima") of his Third String Quartet, op. 94. The critics are unanimous in describing this work as a masterpiece and calling it his last artistic testament, worthy of comparison with the last string quartets of Beethoven.[37] In short, quality and quantity seem decidedly separable in these few last works.

The critics are also in agreement that these final works are all "somberly coloured by reflections on death," in Peter Evans's description, but (as he goes on to say) they "remain wonderfully free from the hysteria of over-emphasis."[38] Britten's letters of this period again give us a clue to the reasons for that lack of overemphatic hysteria. His extreme fatigue and restricted physical activity forced him to face his premature aging in part because they made him face his mortality. "When does aging begin?" asks Gottfried Benn in his essay "Artists and Old Age." His answer is: with the "foreknowledge of early death [which] compensates, in terms of inner life, for decades of outer life and the process of ageing that goes with them."[39] Britten knew he was dying and was not distressed by this fact; a spiritual but not religious man, he came to terms with his mortality.[40] One of the means of doing this may have been through the themes he chose for his last works. In these, Britten shifts away from his heretofore dominant dual thematic focus on the isolated outsider figure and innocence betrayed— the themes of *Peter Grimes, Billy Budd,* and so many other works. Arguably his move from these to the themes of death and dying had come already with that last opera, *Death in Venice,* in which an aging artist, Gustav von Aschenbach, learns about creativity, love, and death. In fact, this opera (unlike the Thomas Mann novella on which it is based) opens with Aschenbach in the throes of a crisis of creativity. This story is usually seen as one of an older man's homoerotic desire for a beautiful boy, and it most certainly is that.[41] But there is another story being told here along with that one, a story about creativity and aging that is very much a response by Britten to the challenges to the second of his life narratives: himself as eternally youthful.

THE LURE OF YOUTH

In order to understand how these two themes of homoerotic desire and creativity/aging come together in the opera, we need to address another, somewhat more controversial aspect of Britten's life: his attraction to the company of young boys. He was often deeply in love, but never sexually involved (to anyone's explicit knowledge), with a series of boys, a topic sensitively dealt with in John Bridcut's film and book *Britten's Children.*[42] With each he had a "mentoring relation suffused with constantly sublimated desire."[43] As one of his biographers tactfully put it: "Despite a long and happy relationship with the tenor Peter Pears, [Britten] found another happiness in the company of boys."[44] We know from his letters and journals that Britten, from an early adult age, delighted in being with children, writing in his early twenties: "I am lost without some children (of either sex) near me."[45] The young composer's own schoolboyish tastes, sense of humor, and general demeanor led one friend to suggest in 1937, "He really hates growing up & away from a very happy childhood that ended only with his Mother's death last Christmas."[46] But it seems clear that this idealized nostalgia for the spontaneity and innocence of the world of his youth continued throughout Britten's life and formed the core of his second life narrative; the corollary to this, of course, was his sensitivity to any threats to that innocence and spontaneity.

That this kind of prolonged nostalgia was not unproblematic is made clear by the playwright Alan Bennett in his play about Britten and Auden, *The Habit of Art* (2009), when he has the older Britten, in 1972, quote back to Auden the poet's actual letter to him from thirty years earlier: "Wherever you go and whatever you do you will always be surrounded by people who adore you, nurse you, praise everything you do, and you build yourself a warm little nest of love by playing the lovable talented little boy."[47] Earlier in the play, Auden put it this way: "Britten was always young. He'll be young now."[48] And in "real life," Bennett was right: until his last years friends constantly commented on Britten's boyish nature and tastes.[49] One friend, Marjorie Fass, tellingly called him a "poor little boy" when he was almost twenty-five and enduring the condescension of certain music critics.[50]

When he did turn twenty-five, the composer lamented to a young friend: "It's a horrible thing to feel one's youth slipping o-so surely away from one & I had such a damn good youth too."[51] His various biographers have traced this desire to retain his "damn good youth" in many different ways throughout his adult life, from preferring "nursery food" to delighting in "childish" card games, from using Lett's Schoolboy's Pocket Diaries to taking cold baths, as he had in school.[52] Perhaps even his desire to live on England's east coast suggests a wish to retain contact with his childhood home. His constant "sportiness"—that is, his competitiveness and pleasure in physical exertion—was seen by his friend, the director Colin Graham, as a desire to "keep the physical side of his youth going" because he was "besotted by youth, and he tried to maintain it in his own life until the day he died."[53] Like being a working composer, being youthful was a central narrative in Britten's life.

His early interest in writing music for children's voices (e.g., *Saint Nicolas* [1947–48]), especially for the unbroken voices of boy trebles, could be seen as part of this same nostalgic youthfulness narrative. As Jonathan Keates expressed it, "For the childless Benjamin Britten, childhood and its enchantments furnished some of his profoundest inspirations as a composer."[54] Others have seen the boys as being Britten's muses, opening up new emotional worlds, and have argued that his preoccupation with the world of childhood gave him "access to areas of the imagination, even to types of music, that he would perhaps not otherwise have approached."[55] Recovering from a bout of depression in 1949, he joyfully turned to writing *The Little Sweep*, an opera for children. Earlier he had composed *The Young Person's Guide to the Orchestra* (1945). Throughout his life he would write not only for children's enjoyment, but also for the child's voice, refusing to "write down" to his young performers. Over the years Britten composed works of both quality and quantity for children's edification and entertainment.[56] He also kept the child, the innocent child, at the forefront of his sung narratives (*Peter Grimes*, *The Turn of the Screw*, *Abraham and Isaac*, *The Golden Vanity*, *Children's Crusade*, *Who Are These Children?*, and *Curlew River*).[57]

And children reciprocated, as the conductor Charles Mackerras noticed: "Children really loved him and were fascinated by him, and by the fact that he spoke their language and, in a way, entered their world."[58] As another friend noted, he changed when around children: "It was almost a return to his own youth, . . . but a kind of idealized image of himself at the age of ten or twelve, the gay, attractive, charming young Lowestoft boy, unerringly skilful in the use of a cricket bat or a tennis racket, and being able to do things with a ball that no other child of his age could do."[59] Indeed, the prepubescent years—the ones before innocence becomes either self-conscious or threatened—appear to figure as the idyllic, if not mythic, ones for Britten. And it was when he was in contact with young adolescents of this age that he was said to be "at his most generous and natural. . . . Through them he re-encountered and re-charged himself."[60] The prepubescent boy was what psychologists might call Britten's "imago"— "the idealized personification of the self that functions as a protagonist of his life narrative."[61] For a person with this self-understanding, to suddenly "age" after surgery would have been even more devastating than it might be for others.

There is little doubt that the company of children was what he always preferred, but this may have been more than just a repressed and sublimated sexual interest for this "Peter Pan composer who would never lose touch with his boyishness."[62] No wonder he was dismayed at, not to say gloomy about, the celebrations in 1963 of his fiftieth birthday.[63] But along with age came changes that were hard to ignore, given both of his life narratives. In a BBC interview, he said, "It is becoming, as I get older, more and more difficult to satisfy my ear that I have found the right notes to express my ideas with."[64] His friends confirm that as he grew older "he seemed to harbour increasing doubts about his own works."[65] Within another decade he would also admit that with age came not only greater expectations and thus demands made by the composer on himself, but also, with success, came greater expectations on the part of both audiences and critics. His 1971 opera for television, *Owen Wingrave,* was both hailed as proof that Britten was "at the masterly height of his career as a composer" and yet deemed "not as masterly an achievement" as the earlier *Turn of the Screw.*[66] And over the years Britten's preperformance nerves when performing on the piano became almost incapacitating. As he explained to a young pianist, "It gets much worse the more famous you become—you have to prove yourself from the first note."[67]

Because of his youthful self-identifying narrative, Britten appears to have been excruciatingly sensitive to the idea of his aging. At the opening of Britten's theater at the Maltings in Snape, Prince Philip innocently asked Tony Palmer, who was filming the proceedings for the BBC: "What's the old man written for us this time?" The fifty-four-year-old Britten was furious—the word "old" enraged him.[68] Less than a decade later the composer made his abrupt entry into "old old age" after his stroke and the increased heart failure. Though his physical decline was visible to all, he attempted to retain his image of himself as almost an eternal schoolboy, but this time with his nurse, Rita Thomson, in the role of the nanny or matron; she, in turn, would describe the ailing Britten as "the best brought-up little boy you could imagine."[69] But he is said to have broken down when hearing the BBC broadcast of *Paul Bunyan* in 1976 when he heard the words of Auden's libretto, "The campfire embers are black and cold, / the banjos are broken, the stories are told, / The woods are cut down and the young are grown old."[70]

ASCHENBACH AND BRITTEN:
THE AGING ARTISTS IN CRISIS

It is here that the protagonist of *Death in Venice* and the aging and ailing composer meet once again—in that opera's second story about aging and creativity. Aschenbach, the respected mature writer, sings "My mind beats on," words suggesting movement and energy.[71] But he sings them to music that is "repetitious, non-developing."[72] This lack of movement is all too fitting, for his next line is "and no words come." As Kildea notes, "Never before had Britten packed so much narrative weight into the opening line of an opera."[73] The aging artist is facing a creative crisis: his mind may "beat on" but it is "taxing, tiring, / unyielding, unproductive."[74] What creativity has meant before this to the writer is, in his own words, "self-discipline" and "routine," his imagination "servant" to his will.[75] In short, "passion" has now left him, and he frets: "I must not betray by any sign of flagging inspiration."[76] As he goes on to lament, the "light of inspiration" has abandoned him, and one might well argue that the reason for this can be discovered in his very welcoming of what he later calls the "austere demands of maturity."[77] The son of a bourgeois father and a bohemian mother, over time Aschenbach has, in his words, "turned away from the paradox and daring of my youth, renounced bohemianism and sympathy with the out-cast soul, to concentrate upon simplicity, beauty, form—upon that all my art is built."[78] This directly echoes Mann's novella; but there would have been another, more personal echo for Britten.

In the same 1942 letter cited by Bennett in his play, Auden had declared to Britten that all great art was the result of "a perfect balance between Order and Chaos, Bohemianism and Bourgeois Convention. Bohemian chaos alone ends in a mad jumble of beautiful scraps. Bourgeois Convention alone ends in large unfeeling corpses. Every artist except the supreme masters has a bias one way or the other. . . . Technical skill always comes from the bourgeois side of one's nature." Since Auden saw Britten as leaning toward the bourgeois, he went on: "Your attraction to thin-as-a-board juveniles, i.e. to the sexless and innocent, is a symptom of this. And I'm certain too that it is your denial and evasion of the demands of disorder that is responsible for your attacks of ill-health, i.e. sickness is your substitute for the Bohemian."[79] The eerie echoing of Mann's split bohemian/bourgeois artist figure might alert us to Britten's investment in this particular story, and not only because of the homosocial nature of the topic: the work was composed as his own health deteriorated and he, the eternal youth, faced premature "aging."

In the operatic version of the story, Achenbach's "maturity"—in other words, his age—is at the heart of the creative crisis that opens the work. The aging writer has premonitions of death from the very start. He decides to go to Venice while walking by a Munich graveyard "the silent graveyard,/ and the silent dead"—and meditating upon what he calls "the black rectangular hole in the ground."[80] Once he arrives in Venice, he rides to the Lido in a gondola and ruminates: "How black a gondola is— / black, coffin black, / a vision of death itself / and the last silent voyage."[81] It is rowed by a bizarre gondolier who is explicitly likened to Charon propelling the writer across the Styx to the world of the dead.

Besides thoughts of death, reminders of age confront Aschenbach. On the boat on his way to Venice, he meets a group of boisterous youths, among them what he calls a "young-old horror"[82]—a character the libretto designates as the Elderly Fop. In youthful clothes and garish makeup that help him mimic (or parody) the young, this character comes back to haunt Aschenbach. At this point the prim and very proper writer is totally appalled by this figure. Later in the opera, however, Aschenbach allows the Hotel Barber to help him "make a stand against advancing years," as the text puts it. He dyes his hair to remove the gray and adds color to his cheeks "to bring back the appearance of youth." The Barber's final words are: "Now the Signore can fall in love with a good grace."[83] That Aschenbach has become the very image of the Elderly Fop is clear both visually and then verbally and musically, as he echoes fragments of the songs of the youths and the "young-old horror" on the boat. That Britten disapproved is equally clear in his distancing from this parody of youthfulness. His discomfort with any stereotypical gay male social behavior is also manifest in his letters, and his biographers stress his social conformism and "middle-class normality" models.[84]

Aschenbach, however, falls in love with a young and beautiful boy whom he can only see through the Hellenizing lenses of Platonic philosophy (and thus ancient Greek homoeroticism): for someone like Britten "to whom the beauty of childhood meant so much, the appropriation of this philosophy would be virtually intuitive."[85] But Plato isn't the only philosopher called upon in both the novella and the opera: Friedrich Nietzsche's famous argument (in *The Birth of Tragedy from the Spirit of Music*) of the aesthetic need to balance Dionysian passion with Apollonian order comes into the foreground as the controlled, restrained artist loses that balance and surrenders to the once (dangerously) repressed Dionysian. It is this, as much as cholera, that brings about his death. Britten, whatever his dark personal struggles, never lost that balance, and the result is the opera *Death in Venice*. The ending of the piece can be read in strongly opposing ways, either as "a scene of denial and pessimism" or, as we would argue, as the sublime reassertion of balance and order through the music,[86] music that has been described as "the most exquisite, most Mahlerian, utterance of Britten's entire output, Aschenbach's and Tadzio's motifs at last meshed together . . . [in] a work of searing brilliance and originality, his power undiminished."[87] Britten's own creativity, in other words, may actually have been nourished by his sublimation, and by those two very different life narratives, both of which came under threat at this time.

LATE STYLE: ADAPTING TO IMPAIRMENT

During the years Britten was composing this opera about aging, creativity, and death, he was himself unwell. To make matters worse, it has been argued, Britten also felt his position as the preeminent English composer was being challenged. With people such as Michael Tippett around, some felt Britten's primarily tonal, if original, music was—while very much his own—now rather old-fashioned.[88] As John Bridcut's film *Britten's Endgame* argues, the "new progressives" found his music too easy, too accessible.[89] It is perhaps not accidental that he was attracted to Mann's novella about aging and creativity for what he himself felt was going to be his last opera—and not only for reasons of sexual politics.

In these final years, part of the composer's coming to terms with his own mortality involved dealing with the loss of those near him as well. In the first weeks after his surgery, in fact, he had to face the deaths of a number of close friends and contemporaries: Auden, Plomer, Dmitri Shostakovich. For an artist like Britten, the life narratives, now necessary for coping with illness and loss, for charting meaning in his life,[90] would have to be adapted. One way of seeing how that adaptation process may have operated is to look at the stories he chose to tell in his last creative works. For instance, *Canticle V* is a setting of T. S. Eliot's obscure early poem "The Death of Saint Narcissus," and, like Mann's novella, it offers what one critic calls "erotic and sexual desire . . . conflated with spiritual longing [that] . . . can find their resolution only through death."[91] Death certainly haunts the last works. The last of the eight medieval lyrics that make up *Sacred and Profane*, op. 91, is called "A Death," and its catalog of the horrors of the end—misty eyes, slack face, running spittle, trembling heart, shaking hands, stiffening feet—is set by Britten with what Kennedy calls "grisly relish": "A great cry of 'All too late! All too late! When the bier is at the gate' momentarily wipes the wry smile from our lips, but Britten does not want our sympathy—the last line is a defiant 'For the whole world I don't care a jot.'"[92]

The next year, 1975, "his renewed creativity reached its peak," claims one of his biographers, while another calls this his "Indian summer."[93] Britten composed *Phaedra*, a solo cantata for mezzo-soprano and chamber orchestra based on Robert Lowell's translation of Racine's play *Phèdre*, for Janet Baker. The cantata takes the awareness of death "untouched by self-pity" as its moving theme, with its protagonist asserting, "I want to die. Death will give me freedom; oh it's nothing not to live; death to the unhappy's no catastrophe!"[94] This "opera-in-miniature,"[95] as it has been called, packs all the emotion of a full operatic work into a mere fifteen minutes. Physically unable to compose an opera, perhaps, because of the restricted spans of creative activity now possible, Britten here made that limitation into a strength. Critics have insisted that "there is no hint of a fatally ill composer husbanding his resources, rather of one eagerly responding to new stimuli" with new sounds in his music.[96] Although that is the case, the same brevity characterizes *Canticle V*, the shortest of the canticles, coming in at about seven minutes in performance.

At this point in his life, as Britten told Alan Blyth in an interview for the *Times*, "writing even a bar or two is a sweat."[97] Rita Thomson was more specific in her description of his new daily routine: "In the mornings he had his breakfast upstairs in bed, and then I would bath and shave him, and dress him. If he had to do it himself, he could have, but then he would have had no energy left over for anything else—he tired very easily. He'd come downstairs at about eleven, and have a beer or something, and then perhaps he'd see Rosamund [Strode] and work with her, or he would work by himself until lunchtime, usually in the drawing room with a little board on his knee."[98] Afternoons were spent in bed, but he would resume work at tea time. As she put it: "He was always working; he worked all the time. The will to work was there. It was the physical part that wasn't so easy."[99] Like the shift from composing for the piano to the harp, this apparently negative constriction of both energy and time actually became a positive, offering a new creative impetus within the narrative of the working composer. The same is true for the shift to the thematics of death and dying. All were arguably productive adaptations (both creative and psychological) to those life narratives challenged by physical change. Facing with courage his decline and imminent death, Britten in a sense mined his life-and-death situation for his art. But age and illness had increasingly rendered mute the youthful life narrative; it was the working-composer narrative that saved the day, the one that was instrumental in mood repair, as psychologists say life narratives can be.[100] It was also this narrative that allowed him to finish "tying up loose ends": in the last four years of his life he produced that last opera and a final song cycle for Pears, a last canticle, a final orchestral piece, a choral work, a cantata for a friend, and a final string quartet that has been seen as offering "a special coda" to the opera.[101]

Because, as we have seen in the first chapter, late style is a matter of reception, critics cannot resist seeing and hearing in these last works the "style" of a dying man. But what they mean by "style" is never clear: sometimes it is thematic, while at other times it is formal, or even a matter of a perceived tone or mood. Whatever it is, as we have noted, it is always an interpretation, a projection, in a way, of the *critic* who knows these are the last works. The same is true of Britten's biographers. For instance, one writes of the *Suite on English Folk Tunes*, op. 90: "The suite is undeniably poignant, its sound irradiated by those strange luminosities which, like the light of the dying sun, reflected from the score of *Death in Venice*. Sorrow for what can never be, love for all that has been, are in this music."[102] Britten's very last work, a short piece for young people's chorus and orchestra called the *Welcome Ode*, op. 95, has been interpreted as his final attempt "to recapture the lost youth and innocence he so desired,"[103] and as offering "one of his strongest moral legacies: enjoy summertime, youth, innocence, and health while they are yours because all too soon they are taken away."[104]

Is this Britten's final message? Perhaps. But it has been a message stated throughout the composer's oeuvre, though now tinged with poignancy at the necessity of bidding farewell to the life narrative of the eternally young boy. What is certainly clear is that right up to the end Britten was totally engaged not only in his own work—that is, in his continuing creativity—but also in the business and artistic affairs of the Aldeburgh Festival, which he had founded in his Suffolk hometown.[105] A few days before he died he presented his friend Mstislav Rostropovich with the sketch of *Praise We Great Men*, one of the few "working" obligations he did not manage to fulfill; as Michael Oliver suggests, "Even at this stage Britten's physical exhaustion was not accompanied by any enfeeblement of his imaginative powers."[106] At his death, Pears said: "There was no struggle to keep alive . . . his greatest feeling was sadness and sorrow at the thought of leaving . . . his friends and his responsibilities."[107]

THE ENDURING AND ENABLING LIFE NARRATIVE

Experiencing as an enforced version of older age the results of the incapacitation caused by his stroke and the greatly diminished energy caused by his progressive heart failure, the composer who wanted to be forever youthful had become suddenly impaired—and, in his own (always young) mind, suddenly old—in his late fifties. Britten died at the age of only sixty-three, not old by the standards of a Strauss or a Verdi or a Tippett. One of his last exchanges with his sister emphasized his longing for death—because of his inability to continue to work. He wrote: "If this is it, and I am sure it is, I want to go. I can't bear to go on any longer not being able to do all the things I used to do."[108] Becoming the first British composer to receive a peerage raised his spirits somewhat in his last year, helping him to get beyond, in his friend Donald Mitchell's words, his feeling of being "ill . . . isolated—and forgotten," no longer "the fashionable composer."[109] Many artists may end their lives feeling somewhat out of step with the innovations of the moment, of course. Some care; some do not. What we think is important to understanding what Britten's late creativity might mean is not this career despondency, but rather his creative adapting of his working life narrative to his changed circumstances. Physical infirmity and disability had to be dealt with; happily, cognitive decline did not. But the narrative of eternal youthfulness did not—could not—evolve with time and had to be discarded.[110]

Britten never literally aged into old age, but he did experience prematurely some of the kinds of challenges that aging brings. In fact, what he did was adapt to these challenges by engaging in what the gerontologist Paul B. Baltes calls "selective optimization with compensation."[111] One famous example of this kind of adaptation would be that of the pianist Arthur Rubenstein: as he aged Rubenstein said he reduced his repertoire and played a smaller number of pieces (selection); he practiced these more often (optimization); and he slowed down his speed of playing prior to fast movements, so that the contrast would enhance the impression of speed in those fast movements (compensation).[112] For Britten, the parallel process would have been his choosing to write a smaller number of works, and those on a smaller scale; the optimization consisted of conserving his limited physical and mental energies for composition; and the compensation for his stroke impairment would include everything from composing for the harp instead of the piano to cutting the music sheets in half so he could reach to the top or composing a string quartet because it needed only four staves of music, at a time when he had no energy to complete a page of full score.[113] The results of this "selective optimization with compensation" was a creative output that is smaller, but not different in terms of style or, most agree, quality; the last works were still composed in what is thought of as his characteristic mode of musical expression, in this case a mix of his sparer and simpler style of the late 1950s and early 1960s and his virtuosic earlier works.[114]

For Britten's recent biographer Paul Kildea, "instead of decline . . . these [last] were years of unfettered brilliance, of inspiration at every turn and of notebooks brimming with plans and ideas."[115] Those adaptations to his life narrative as a professional working composer, a creator, were what saw him through to the end. With impairment, however, came the necessary failure of the other narrative. Christopher Palmer rightly notes that "when Britten's enchanted childhood yielded to adolescence and maturity there 'pass'd away a glory from the earth' which he sought in vain to recapture throughout his adult life. It is a fact of life that the childhood vision, once clouded over, can never be recaptured in its pristine purity; a fact of life that Britten was never able to come to terms with."[116] However, physical impairment, in the end, meant the impossibility of any recapturing of youth. While Palmer believes that "Britten's child-like-ness was the mainspring of his creativity,"[117] we would argue that this was only one of the life narratives that made Britten the productive creator he was—and continued to be—even after his sudden entry into "old old age": his dedication to his creative work and his self-identifying as a "working" composer provided the sustaining other narrative.

CHAPTER SEVEN

Conclusion: The Particularities
of Aging and Creativity

It is difficult enough to make convincing models to account for the ev-
eryday behavior and activity of people who we might describe, rightly
or wrongly, as "normal"—how much more difficult, and perhaps even
fruitless, to make generalizations about artists whose individuality is
their calling card.
—Michael Beckerman, "Leoš Janáček and 'The Late Style' in Music"

In exploring the lives of these four composers, we were struck by how,
as they aged, their creativity functioned—and how differently it functioned—in helping them adapt to the very individual personal situations
of their later years. To see whether the same might hold true for other
composers as well, we decided to look at the lives of a selection of composers from the same period with very different lives and careers, whose
last years and late creativity have been studied in detail by other scholars:
the Russian Sergei Prokofiev, the Czech Leoš Janáček, the German Hans
Werner Henze, the Australian Peggy Glanville-Hicks, the Finn Jean Sibelius, and the British Ethel Smyth. And once again, as shall be evident in
this chapter, we discovered that the particularities of their lives, personal
circumstances, and creative habits precluded any easy generalization. For
some of them, as for Verdi, Strauss, Messiaen, and Britten, creativity was
indeed closely associated with aspects of their personhood that were significant in forging for themselves the individual sustaining narratives of
their lives. Nevertheless, we also discovered, for each of the four and for
some of the others, periods of affective distress related to or interfering
with their creative activity—though it was often creativity that ultimately
was of importance in overcoming that distress. In concluding, we want
to return to our four composers' last creative works and ask whether they

could constitute *Vollendungsopern*, that is, "completion operas," for the works' protagonists and for the composers who created them.

CREATIVITY AND PERSONHOOD

In chapter 1 we saw that according to a prominent theory in psychology today, we all construct life narratives for ourselves to give our lives unity, meaning, and purpose. While these are not necessarily accessible to the rest of the world, the external image that we present to the outside world is, and that too is always the result of a process of construction. As we age, this act of self-fashioning becomes the creation of a last and, we hope, lasting identity, one that is public, though it obviously may also reflect the private.

Whether individual artists choose to continue to be creative in their last years depends very much on the role creativity plays in their sense of themselves as persons and their construction of that life narrative (at least, when continuing to work isn't simply a matter of financial survival). As we have seen with both Britten and Strauss, some composers have to keep creating, for it is essential to their identities. Others need to extend themselves at the end: Messiaen chose to compose his first opera as both an extension and a summation of a lifetime of musical innovations and religious belief. Jacques Offenbach felt he had to respect his talent by composing in his last years not only operettas (which came easily) but also a serious dramatic opera (which did not). But Gioachino Rossini (1792–1868) obviously felt differently: he happily retired from the opera stage at the age of thirty-eight, a successful and wealthy composer of some thirty-nine operas.

The career of Sergei Prokofiev (1891–1953), however, makes it clear that both health and external circumstances can intervene negatively in an artist's late creativity, even when the desire to continue creating is strong. When the émigré composer returned from Paris to Stalinist Russia in 1936, he was in his forties; the next decade and a half would see his health decline, his political and financial standing rise and then fall precipitously, and his confidence crash. Though his compositions changed over these years, his creativity remained undiminished, as he spent his remaining time and energy in an attempt to assure his musical legacy. Simon Morrison's extensive research into the composer's sealed files in the Russian State Archives, presented in *The People's Artist: Prokofiev's Soviet Years* (2009), has yielded a portrait of a man who died in his early sixties but spent a decade suffering from chronic high blood pressure that often rendered him bedridden with debilitating headaches and nosebleeds. In 1949, following a stroke, he was told to rest and forbidden to compose. But his doctor finally agreed to let him return to his work, saying, "One cannot keep an artist from creating." She feared that if he didn't write, his "moral and psychological state" would worsen.[1]

These same years were also years of great artistic stress, as the makers of Russian cultural policy repeatedly thwarted Prokofiev's attempts to have his monumental opera *War and Peace* staged in its entirety, making him cut and modify the score and text extensively. He endured an official censure in 1948, in part because his music was deemed modernist, an example of "decadent distortion," even though he attempted to comply with demands for socialist realist content, as he did in his opera *A Story of a Real Man*. For reasons of financial need and political pragmatism, he found himself accepting commissions for official Soviet celebrations. The real struggle in his last years was one to preserve his artistic integrity and independence. Despite the loss of creative agency that came from both his unstable health and the need to appease the cultural ideologues, what Morrison calls Prokofiev's "irrepressible creative passion" continued in the face of the deaths of friends and colleagues, increasing bureaucratic interference, and frequent declines in his self-confidence.[2] His last works, however, are characterized by what Morrison calls "a decline in melodic, harmonic, and rhythmic invention that reflects the parameters of his commissions and the difficulties he had concentrating as his health continued to deteriorate."[3] Muting "his creative voice," he turned to self-recycling—a move Morrison sees as a form of self-censorship.[4] This was no Straussian musical life review, in other words; it was more a means of survival.

That said, there are more fortunate artists who not only continue into a much older age than Prokofiev managed, but indeed flourish. Michael Beckerman's insightful study of the later life and last works of the Czech composer Leoš Janáček (1854–1928) uses a series of expressive words to describe what happened in the last ten years of this artist's life: "a tumultuous crescendo of power and mastery," "creative spurt," "eruption," "comet."[5] Indeed, Janáček is remembered today in large part for the works he wrote in his last years. The usual story is that his love for a younger woman was the inspiration, but Beckerman puts this in the broader life context of the composer's retirement from teaching, a lifetime of "hard work, relentless struggle, and deep concentration," and finally the birth of modern Czechoslovakia and his recognition at long last as a national composer.[6]

We have seen that the vicissitudes of aging demand adaptations of life narratives so that they can continue to serve their integrating functions. Yet, an argument can be made that creative artists in particular, because of expectations (their own and others'), may not be allowed to easily reconfigure their narratives of purpose and coherence—simply because they *are* artists. Most people adjust their personal expectations as they get older, so that they see themselves as the same even as they age: that is, they create a continuous sense of personhood, despite differences.[7] To use a banal but perhaps clarifying example, if one sees oneself as a golfer, at age forty one might have a handicap of four; by age seventy that handicap may be sixteen, but one would have adjusted one's expectations to see this as playing at the same level as before. Robert Atchley's continuity theory of aging "views the individual as motivated to preserve and maintain existing internal and external structures" and so is "not merely reactive or adaptive in doing so, but actively employs a variety of strategies to enhance continuity."[8] But what happens when those personal expectations to be adjusted are not under their control, when (as is the case with creative artists) external demands can influence what is expected of them in later life? Famous creative artists, arguably, may not be permitted to adjust their expectations because their audiences are anticipating only progress and ever greater works. And if the artist is perceived as nearing the end of life, does a late-style discourse intervene, and therefore does the audience expect the great summation, the culmination of the career? And if they do not find it, do they then dismiss the artists as past their prime?

Some creative artists, however, attempt to retain control of both the expectations of others and their own life narrative. Some, for example, consider their last works the most mature, and thus the most significant—and say so. They therefore consciously attempt to orchestrate, so to speak, their own "model of career closure" through what has been called "testamentary acts."[9] Such self-fashioning allows them to try to exert posthumous control over their artistic reputations. While alive, they may resist the *critics'* attempts to structure their life narratives for them—for example, by periodizing their careers. When asked at the age of seventy whether he saw the pattern in his life as being in three periods, like Beethoven's, Messiaen replied that he did not, for he had never "renounced" his past and always looked to the future, thanks to his career teaching young people with new ideas at the Paris Conservatoire.[10]

What about composers who construct their own lateness but are fooled by time, when they live longer than they expected—as we have seen occurred with Messiaen? Hans Werner Henze (1926–2012) wrote in 1998 about his fantasy of finishing his opera *Venus und Adonis* in 1995: "All that would be left of me would be an exhausted, tired old husk with a mind that was sensitive to noise and a body sensitive to pain and a wholly justified need for a couple of glasses of the new year's wine."[11] Yet he lived on and created for a goodly number of years, finishing his operatic career with *L'Upapa und der Triumph der Sohnesliebe* (2003), for which he wrote both libretto and score. This fanciful opera—parodying as it does everything from Mozart to Wagner to Messiaen—invoked in the critical response much familiar (and positive) late-style discourse. It was considered "the summation of long experience—his *Zauberflöte*, his *Tempest*, perhaps his farewell to the world."[12] A similar fate faced Tippett: he set up the large-scale choral work *The Mask of Time* (1984) as the high point of his late style, along with his Fourth Symphony, but this plan "was subsequently negated by the accident of remaining alive, and creatively active, for more than a decade longer."[13] Hence the need to reinvent his own late self-fashioning.

It is equally clear, however, that some artists cannot continue to be creative—for any number of reasons. Peggy Glanville-Hicks (1912–1990) was a successful, much commissioned, and award-winning creator of four operas and many other compositions, from ballets to concertos. But she had to spend much of her time writing *about* music, rather than composing it, in order to pay the rent, for she faced financial challenges for most of her life. Her final opera, *Sappho*, written in 1963 and based on Lawrence Durrell's verse play, was intended to celebrate the return of Maria Callas to the operatic stage, this time as a mezzo-soprano. But the San Francisco Opera (which commissioned the piece) rejected it, and it was not recorded until 2012.[14] What cut short the composer's career, shortly after this in 1967, was surgery for a life-threatening brain tumor that impaired her sight. Losing her sense of smell after the surgery, and with her eyesight continuing to fail, she too faced impairment in ways that recall Britten's last years, but for her, this period lasted a much longer time: she lived another twenty-four years and seems to have composed only one three-minute piece, *Girondelles for Giraffes* (1978), in those years.[15]

Perhaps the most famous example of the silencing of creativity with age is not a composer of operas, but an important composer nonetheless: Finland's national musical icon, Jean Sibelius (1865–1957). Retreating to his isolated home in the Finnish countryside in 1927, he published nothing major for the last thirty years of his life and burned a good number of his manuscript scores in 1945. Turning to alcohol to stop his hand tremor and to keep his relentless self-criticism at bay, he claimed in these years to have a continuing "fascination" with composing, a fascination "bound up with the difficulty of the task." He continued: "Let no one imagine that composing is easier for an old composer if he takes his art seriously. The demands one makes on oneself have increased in the course of years. Greater sureness make[s] one scorn solutions that come too easily, that follow the line of least resistance, in a higher degree than formerly. One is always faced with new problems. The thing that has pleased me most is that I have been able to reject. The greatest labor that I have expended, perhaps, was on works that have never been completed."[16] One of those works was his Eighth Symphony—never finished and likely burned in 1945. Given the composer's belief that each of his symphonies must have its own different technique, one that had to be "lived through" by its creator,[17] and given, as well, the intensely critical self-scrutiny evident in his journals, it is perhaps no surprise that this work was never completed. For almost thirty years Sibelius would become irritated, even angry, when questions arose, as they did constantly, about its completion. The pressure on him came not only from the work's commissioner and the two orchestras that had first-performance rights, but also from legions of journalists, music critics, and even ordinary fans all over the world.[18]

Among the most importuning of these was the *New York Times* music critic Olin Downes, who had in effect appropriated Sibelius for his own cause. He made him into the wholesome, virile, yet spiritual hero who could combat modernism—what Downes presented as that un-American, bloodless, "geometrical music" of Schoenberg and the emotionless, intellectual abstraction of Stravinsky.[19] The modernist position on Sibelius was voiced in 1938 by Theodor Adorno in an excoriating attack on him for being the opposite of the "advanced New Music," calling his work an "incomprehensible whole made up of the most trivial details [that] produces the false image of profundity."[20] It was not that Sibelius was ever unaware of the "New Music"; on the contrary, he kept up with younger composers' work. After a two-month trip to Berlin as early as 1910, however, he had written: "As usual I acquired an unconquerable distaste for the 'modern tendency.'"[21] But in the end, according to one of his biographers, the ever self-critical composer "saw his own limitations in regard to particular skills";[22] his creativity was never stimulated by systematized theories but instead by nature, much to Adorno's disgust. According to Sibelius's secretary, in his last years he remained disturbed by new tendencies in music, for he saw himself as representing the past in a changed world.[23]

Sibelius's long silence in his long older age clearly had many contributing factors. He had outlived his generation. He was painfully obsessed with the Eighth Symphony in the face of the immense (and intense) expectations of others, but even more so in the face of his own increasing expectations of himself and thus his increasing self-censorship. The horrors of World War II, he said, "make me mentally and physically sick. That is one of the reasons why I have not created anything in more than twenty years that I could have offered to the public with an easy heart."[24] His works continued to be popular (especially in the United States and Great Britain), and with that success came the pressures of worldwide celebrity—the demands and expectations of official visitors, journalists, photographers, fans. This success with audiences sat uncomfortably, for him, beside his dismissal by the modernists and their apologists as having outlived his time and being a relic of a bygone age.[25] He had always been known to be prone to insecurity, lack of confidence, and depression; did such multiple and complex pressures lead to the willed silencing of his creativity or to an extended and paralyzing creative despondency?

THE "LATER-LIFE CRISIS" AND AGING CREATORS

Depressive symptoms and depression itself are not, we are told, uncommon in older individuals, and are seen to be related to the stress of accumulated negative life events and the changes, neuroanatomic and physical, that age may bring.[26] The four composers whose lives we examined experienced periods of depressive symptoms that made continuing creativity difficult, and in each case these were associated with their advancing age and either their health or their particular life circumstances. They had times when they felt their later life to be oppressive, when the weight of their years seemed hard to bear. Inevitably, these were moments when things seemed beyond their control, when their agency was compromised. We see these periods as the outcomes of sometimes prolonged threats to their sense of personhood and wonder if they could be considered a kind of "later-life crisis."

The related phrase "late-life crisis" has become a cliché today, used in the popular media to describe anything seemingly inappropriate done in older age—from acquiring a tattoo to applying for a motorcycle license. The term is modeled, obviously, upon "mid-life crisis," coined by Elliott Jaques in 1965.[27] This influential label designated a depressive crisis, experienced around the age of thirty-five, that could lead to mature adulthood and the sense of serenity that come from the accepting and transcending of the inevitability of death and the destructive impulses within each of us. Though Jaques mentions two crises at the start of his paper, one at thirty-five and the other at sixty-five, he never addresses the latter. It is with the earlier one that he associates a sense of aging and mortality: "The individual has stopped growing up, and has begun to grow old"; it is death, "one's own real and actual mortality," that is said to precipitate the critical nature of this earlier stage.[28] Arguably, however, a crisis at around sixty-five years, what we could call a "later-life crisis," may be more likely, given the even greater proximity of mortality and the more likely threats to personhood posed by issues such as health problems. Or perhaps it might be less the imminence of death than the possibility of dependency and loss of autonomy that present the threat. As Stephen Katz responded to this suggestion, this crisis might mark "the beginning of a sense or vision of the boundary between Third and Fourth ages, its emergence in sometimes disruptive and painful ways, a feeling that this is the beginning of possible ends. For the [four] composers, some of their work seems to be an exercise in reflexive aging."[29] What seems clear is that negotiating a later-life crisis can bring about an adjustment to one's sense of personhood.

This is part of the lesson of Elizabeth Wood's "On Deafness and Musical Creativity: The Case of Ethel Smyth,"[30] which studies with great detail and even greater sympathy both Ethel Smyth's last compositional works and her unpublished responses to the crisis of the onset and progression of deafness. Unlike Beethoven, Smetana, and Fauré, who all continued to compose despite deafness, Smyth found that her hearing difficulties compromised her ability to compose, most obviously when she was in her sixties. In 1919 Smyth wrote to her sister: "Inspiration is difficult because of deafness. . . . It has been settled or ordained for me that the main point of my life can't be worked anymore. [The publisher] Longman's acceptance of my book seems to prove that I have another gift. 'Old Providence' sees fit to turn music away from me (it is not that I am turning from music)."[31]

However, that move from composing to writing would not happen for more than a decade. Despite increasing deafness combined with tinnitus (a perpetual ringing in her ears), and despite self-doubt, depression, and understandable procrastination, Smyth kept writing music, reorchestrating and rearranging earlier works and composing a number of last works, including her fifth opera, *Fête Galante* (1922), a piece that Wood sees as full of echoes of the particular sound world in which Smyth grew up. From this insight, and with the aid of contemporary neuroscience, Wood develops a theory of how Smyth could manage to continue to compose, with the aid of imagination and aural memory and in the face of her severe hearing difficulties, through eight productive years in the 1920s. She finds that these last works are all "about death and sonic remembering, loss and auditory recapitulation. They are all memorials. But the mere fact that she

could write them means they are all about life; about the complicated relationship between death and return; about revivifying the past and defying
death and deafness."[32]

As Smyth entered her seventies, however, she gave up composing for
good: "She boxed up all her scores, made an inventory of all her posses-
sions, and then refused to talk about music or answer questions about
it."[33] She did engage that other "gift," though, and wrote her memoirs over
many years. Her friend Vernon Lee is said to have given Smyth the motto
that got her through life: "One must be prepared to begin life all over again
an unlimited number of times." The composer saw this as meaning that
"as long as breath is in your body life need never cease to be a creative effort."[34] Resilience countered depression; creativity adapted and found new
forms. In a radio broadcast on her eightieth birthday, Smyth insisted that
"if you find your former activities impossible, you must not be passively
resigned to that, but find other activities that are possible."[35] Could such a
"later-life crisis," resolved through acceptance and creative agency, somehow manifest itself in a composer's late works as well?

VOLLENDUNGSOPERN

Another way to pose this question is: could the late or last opera of an aging
composer function as what we might call, after Constance Rooke, a *Vollendungsoper*, that is, a winding-up work, an opera of completion? Rooke
posits the existence of a *Vollendungsroman* as the later-age response to
the *Bildungsroman*, the novel of youthful development. This late-focused
work, for Rooke, has the task of discovering "for its protagonist and for
the reader some kind of affirmation in the face of loss." The felt proximity
of death, she argues, leads an aged protagonist to seize "some affirmation
out of the jaws of death, to discover meaning in the face of nothingness."[36]
If the author is also aging, his or her own life is inevitably involved, thus
leading to both greater intensity and greater detachment, she argues.
In the case of the older composer of an opera, this might influence the
choice of subject, theme, and mode of representation of aging characters
and their particular struggles. The operatic equivalent might well offer the
kind of thematic affirmation Rooke suggests, but we would like to explore
whether it might also signal in the composer himself a coming to terms
with age and mortality with new creative strength.

Janáček's final three operas show the composer doing precisely this in
interesting ways. To return to Beckerman's reading of his late years and
works, we can see how Janáček first turned to the lessons of nature's cycles

as told operatically in an animal fable. In *Příhody lišky Bystroušky* (1924; *The Cunning Little Vixen*), a meditation on youth and age, he significantly expanded the source text (a comic strip) when he wrote his own libretto and had the vixen Bystrouška overtaken by a deadly bullet just as the human Forester was overtaken by the fatigue of older age. But in a dream, the Forester sees a young Bystrouška, the very image of her mother: life goes on and nature continues. In the next opera, *Věc Makropulos* (1926; *The Makropulos Affair*), the protagonist chooses a natural death over an unnatural, extended life (of over three hundred years), asserting strongly that death is what gives life meaning. The last, *Zmrtvého domu* (1927–28, premiered 1930; *From the House of the Dead*), answers the pessimism of Dostoevsky's source text with optimism and hope without losing the Russian's sense of abject human misery. Each of what we would call these last *Vollendungsopern* also ends musically with what Beckerman describes as "a forceful upsweep" and "a grand peroration or a final apotheosis."[37]

In the case of the four composers we studied here in detail, their final works too can be seen as a kind of ego-extension and thus can also be read as part of the process of their late self-fashioning through their life stories. Both Verdi and his rival Wagner consciously created their public narratives of themselves, from early on: Verdi always claimed to be a simple man of the people, an unrecognized early talent, and to some extent a self-taught artist. While little of this was precisely accurate, the narrative fed nicely into Italian romantic nationalism. Similarly, Wagner claimed to be an untutored romantic genius, open to the spirit of the German *Volk*. In short, both self-mythified, and both of their self-myths are arguably ideologically intended. As we have seen, Verdi was no less preoccupied with the Italianness (*italianità*) of his national culture than Wagner was with his conscious, if racist, ideology of the pure German and the Aryan. And at a certain point in their lives, they both saw themselves as late artists and began consciously crafting their own versions of their final identity.

Wagner frequently asserted to anyone who would listen that *Parsifal* would be his last opera, and articulated this inevitable progression in his autobiographical writings. As Anthony Barone explores at length, Wagner carefully constructed his late-style persona.[38] Verdi was equally in control of his later life narratives; indeed, he had several simultaneous and seemingly contradictory ones: the simple farmer and the generous philanthropist, but also the "lion" of the Italian operatic world. Through his last work, *Falstaff*, he wanted to point the way forward, to save the younger Italian composers from being led astray into foreign (that is, Germanic) "symphonism"—far from the core values of Italian opera.

Falstaff's titular roguish, aging protagonist has little to do with Verdi's own personality, though we have seen that several of the lines his librettist gave to Falstaff resonated with the composer's own ways of dealing with the trials of aging: those involved with keeping your sense of humor ("Tutto nel mondo è burla") and with keeping on going ("Va, va, vecchio John"). Falstaff also offered a wonderfully exuberant response to the Wagnerian obsession with degeneration manifested in *Parsifal*: Falstaff is a character for whom regeneration through renunciation of the fleshly pleasures of life is just not on the table. But in addition to the libretto, the music of *Falstaff* offers an affirmation of the composer's artistic self, through its assertion of *italianità* and its lesson for the future offered to the younger Italian composers of his day: change, but be Italian still.

If the late Verdi looked with hope to the future, Strauss could only look backward with great sadness at the end of his life. Like Wagner before him, who incorporated the pessimism of Arthur Schopenhauer in his view of the degeneration of humanity after the ancient world, Strauss saw himself, in the aftermath of World War II, as being at the end of German musical culture as he had known it. Through his musical life review in his later years, he constructed an artistic narrative of his role within his culture's history. *Capriccio* can be seen as a *Vollendungsoper* at the level of the story, where the composer's personal voice is that of the older impresario LaRoche, arguing for the respect of tradition. At the level of the music, as part of that life review, we are given a self-reflexive reprise of the composer's life's work in the context of the history of opera. In those final *Four Last Songs*, however, he turned from the past to his present, affirming his art in the face of death and providing a model for what Rooke calls seizing "some affirmation out of the jaws of death."

Messiaen's self-construction was from the very start as a lay Catholic who was carrying out God's work through his composing, bringing the truths of his religion to audiences in the concert hall and then the opera house. In addition, by agreeing to compose an opera in his last years, he attempted to innovate and change the very genre of opera, hoping to renew it in the process. What he actually did was to create a piece that is unique and inimitable, yet one that because of its very scope and size is always an "occasion" whenever it is performed. *Saint François d'Assise* is certainly an opera about mortality, but its deeply Catholic composer refused to end the opera with the saint's death, instead moving ahead to the spiritual salvation that he hoped would be his own as well. Such clear affirmation in the face of death makes this perhaps the most straightforward of the *Vollendungsopern*.

If this be so, Britten's *Death in Venice* is the least straightforward. Yes, it is an opera about the protagonist's aging, creativity, and death, but there is little affirmation within the staged narrative. It is only the composer for whom there can be any creative affirmation, for, unlike his character, Britten could and did create the balance between destructive Dionysian impulses and Apollonian formal control—in the making of this very opera. By the time he was in his forties Britten had been recognized as the English opera composer his nation had been waiting for. We have argued that the youthfulness narrative that had always sustained him had to be abandoned in the face of his poor health and impairment. What remained was the other strong, parallel life story of the productive, working composer, not only driven to compose to feel alive and continuing to do so to the end, but also directing the thriving Aldeburgh Festival.

While each composer can be said to have ended with a *Vollendungsoper*, those works, like each of their later lives, were unique, supporting the contention that it is "a fruitless distortion to invoke a single motif to capture the variegated images of late life."[39] All four composers, as they aged, remained creative in their own individual ways: no single theory of later-life creativity or late style suffices to characterize their last years and works. While there may be life issues that are shared by aging artists—expectations (their own and others'), intergenerational differences, the probability of dealing with losses—how these are dealt with is resolutely individual within personal situations of both art and life that are unique to each. So too are their last works different, even if each can potentially be seen, in its individual way, as a work of completion. The cliché is that last works share a tone, a mood, usually expressed as "autumnal." Yet for every somber *Four Last Songs* there is a joyous *Falstaff*. The other generalizations about late works often involve thematic concerns and subject matter, especially in the case of texted music such as opera or song: they are said to be about death, aging, memory, acceptance of the follies of humankind, a broader view of life in the face of mortality, introspection leading to self-reflexivity.[40] While this might describe Britten's *Death in Venice*, Michael Tippett's last opera, *New Year* (1989), is in the end resolutely positive and affirmative.

∞

Coming now to the end of our study, we have to ask ourselves: are there, then, any final lessons to be learned from the stories of these musical "old masters"?

The first is the obvious one to which we keep returning: not only that each creative artist is radically individual, but that the changes and challenges of aging come from multiple directions, making it as impossible to generalize about older age as it is about the young. These challenges may be physical, as with Britten, or intergenerational, as with Verdi. They may, on the other hand, come from one's political and social circumstances, as in the case of Strauss. All of these composers lived long enough to have to respond to the "new"—and with modernism came the added imperative of innovation and progress, as seen most prominently in the life of Olivier Messiaen. However, these various challenges of aging turned out to be first threats and then stimulants to the creativity of these composers. In other words, creativity has its costs. It isn't simply a therapeutic answer to a later-life crisis; rather, it is often the cause of the crisis. For these canonic and indeed iconic national composers, fame and success were as much a burden as a blessing. With age and experience came not only greater ambition but also greater expectations. And so their self-fashioning of their late persona was in part conditioned by their worries, different as they were, about their final artistic legacy.

Nevertheless, we have learned something important from the examples of their *Vollendungsopern*, as well as from what we can glean from their self-presentations about their attitudes to their creativity and their own aging in their later years. Smyth said it best: "As long as breath is in your body life need never cease to be a creative effort."

ACKNOWLEDGMENTS

To the late Edward W. Said, who convinced us to take up this project, our gratitude for both the encouragement and the example of his own inspiring late work on late style. When we were invited to speak at the Verdi 2001 conference (at New York and New Haven), it was Edward's provocation and support that prompted our preliminary foray into the debates on late style. We'd like to thank the expert (and immensely generous) respondents to our paper at that time: Carolyn Abbate, Roger Parker, and Emanuele Senici. To Stephen Katz, to whom we wrote a fan letter when we read his book, *Disciplining Old Age*, special thanks for getting (and keeping) us on course through his advice and criticism. Ditto to Anthony Barone, whose insightful and meticulous doctoral dissertation on Wagner and late style has been the mainstay of our thinking in this entire project, as will have been more than clear to readers of this book. He is also the reason there is no Wagner chapter in this book: there is simply nothing more to say.

We are also deeply in debt to the most effective team of research assistants anyone could ever wish for. Over several years we were fortunate enough to work with Kimberly Fairbrother Canton, Amelia DeFalco, Katherine R. Larson, and Helmut Reichenbächer. Their astute research instincts, their deep knowledge of their own scholarly areas, their enthusiasm, and their sheer hard work kept us going through the chapters on Richard Strauss and Benjamin Britten, and their own fine collective publications in these areas acted as models for us. A companion to chapter 6 is a jointly written piece that came out of the team's collective efforts: Kimberly F. Canton, Amelia DeFalco, Linda Hutcheon, Michael Hutcheon, Katherine R. Larson, and Helmut Reichenbächer, "*Death in Venice* and Beyond: Benjamin Britten's Late Works," *University of Toronto Quarterly*

81, no. 4 (2012): 893–908. These scholars were our first and toughest readers. We enjoyed working with them immensely and learned much from
them; now that they are launched on their own various academic careers,
many others will have that pleasure as well. At other moments in the long
process of writing this book, we also had the expert advice and research
assistance of Keith Johnston and Misha Teramura, for which we are deeply
grateful.

Our fellowship at the University of Michigan Humanities Institute
back in 2003 allowed us to plunge into the research on both aging and
creativity in a vibrant collegial environment. That, in turn, prepared us
to apply for and, happily, receive grant support from the Social Sciences
and Humanities Research Council of Canada, without which this project
could never have been completed.

When it was finally finished, the two expert readers who reviewed
it for the University of Chicago Press were the kind of meticulous, engaged, constructive readers that all authors dream of having, and happily
they allowed us to know their identities. Our deepest thanks, therefore,
go to Gordon McMullan, whose own fine work on late style has been an
inspiration to us, and to Michael Beckerman, whose illuminating study
of Janáček's late years both was a model for us and also set the bar very
high. The highly professional Barbara Norton was the press's copy editor
extraordinaire, expertly guiding us with her keen eye and exquisite tact.
And working with our editor Marta Tonegutti was a personal and intellectual delight: her support, encouragement, and critical eye all made this
a better book. Our thanks also go to two other readers (of the entire manuscript) whose creativity and musical knowledge we cherish: Dorothy Glick
and Tim McCracken.

To Lawrence Wiliford, for both his research work at the Britten-Pears
Library and for the inspiration of his wonderful singing of Britten's songs,
goes our gratitude. To Nick Clark, Colin Matthews, and Lucy Walker at
the Britten-Pears Foundation in Aldeburgh, our thanks for their patience,
deep knowledge, and kind assistance. To the late Ian Tait, our thanks for
passing on his medical knowledge of Britten's last years. Stephen Ralls
and Bruce Ubukata shared with us their memories and knowledge of Aldeburgh and graciously offered us their generous response to our group's
research.

The chapter on Olivier Messiaen was written during a blissful fellowship at the Camargo Foundation in Cassis, France. To our fellow fortu-
nates (especially to composer Dan Welcher and Messiaen convert Laura

Manning) and to Connie Higginson and Leon Selig—who kept us working (and playing) so well—go our thanks.

The members of the Working Group on Age–Old Age–Aesthetics of the Jackman Humanities Institute, at the University of Toronto, were our companions in thought throughout the last years of finishing this work. Special thanks go to its leaders, Marlene Goldman and Andrea Charise. Thanks too to the members of the UK-based network Late-Life Creativity and the "New Old Age": Arts and Humanities and Gerontology in Critical Dialogue, whose workshops, website, and intellectual support have been crucial to our last years on this project. Particular thanks to Gordon Mc-Mullan, once again, and Sam Smiles—who together organized the confer-ence Rethinking Late Style: Art, Literature, Music, Film at King's College, London, in November 2007.

Then there is our deep gratitude to those whose work and example (as well as much-needed advice) kept us going over the years: Sander Gilman, Philip Sohm, Kathleen Woodward, Roberta Marvin, Peter Hill, Christo-pher Dingle, and Rosemary Garland Thomson. And we must add to that list those who read parts of the manuscript and gave of both their time and expertise to help us: Caryl Clark, Sherry Lee, Christopher Hailey, Colleen Renihan, Noe Zamel, and Ann Urbancic.

To the many audiences (academic, operatic, medical, and other) who were subjected to parts of this project in talks over the years, our thanks for your patience, engagement, and suggestions. And a special (and not to-tally ironic) debt is owed to the antiquated plumbing systems of two of the world's great library cities—Paris and London—for keeping us waiting for plumbers and writing, writing, writing.

Linda and Michael Hutcheon

CHAPTER ONE

1. http://www.metmuseum.org/collections/search-the-collections/170008299. Accessed 12 December 2012.

2. Woodward quoted from her *Ageing and Its Discontents: Freud and Other Fictions* (Bloomington: Indiana University Press, 1991), 10. For a sampling of scholarship on last works, on visual artists see Erin Campbell, "The Art of Aging Gracefully: The Elderly Artist as Courtier in Early Modern Art Theory and Criticism," *Sixteenth-Century Journal* 33, no. 2 (2002): 321–31; and Philip Sohm, *The Artist Grows Old: The Aging of Art and Artists in Italy, 1500–1800* (New Haven: Yale University Press, 2007). On writers, see Gordon McMullan, *Shakespeare and the Idea of Late Writing: Authorship in the Proximity of Death* (Cambridge: Cambridge University Press, 2007). On musicians, see Maynard Solomon, *Late Beethoven: Music, Thought, Imagination* (Berkeley and Los Angeles: University of California Press, 2003); and Margaret Notley, *Lateness and Brahms: Music and Culture in the Twilight of Viennese Liberalism* (New York: Oxford University Press, 2007).

3. Linda Hutcheon and Michael Hutcheon, *Opera: Desire, Disease, Death* (Lincoln: University of Nebraska Press, 1996); *Bodily Charm: Living Opera* (Lincoln: University of Nebraska Press, 2000); and *Opera: The Art of Dying* (Cambridge, MA: President and Fellows of Harvard College, 2004).

4. Stephen Katz, *Disciplining Old Age: The Formation of Gerontological Knowledge* (Charlottesville: University Press of Virginia, 1996), 18–19.

5. Vern L. Bengtson, Norella M. Putney, and Malcolm L. Johnson, "The Problem of Theory in Gerontology Today," in *The Cambridge Handbook of Age and Ageing*, ed. Malcolm L. Johnson, Vern L. Bengtson, Peter G. Coleman, and Thomas B. L. Kirkwood (Cambridge: Cambridge University Press, 2005), 5.

6. Helen M. Sorenson and James A. Thorson, *Geriatric Respiratory Care* (Albany, NY: Delmar, 1998), 9.

7. Peter Laslett, *A Fresh Map of Life: The Emergence of the Third Age*, 2nd ed. (London: Macmillan, 1995). On the Fourth Age, see Paul B. Baltes and J. Smith, "New

Frontiers in the Future of Aging: From Successful Aging of the Young Old to the Dilem-
mas of the Fourth Age," *Gerontology* 49 (2003): 123–35.

8. Christian Lalive d'Epinay, "Images of Aging in Autobiographical Narratives
of the Elderly," in *Images of Aging in Western Societies: Proceedings of the Second
"Images of Aging" Conference,* ed. Cornelia Hummel and Christian J. Lalive d'Epinay
(Geneva: Centre for Interdisciplinary Gerontology, 1995), 144.

9. See François Höpflinger, "From Agism to Gerontologism? Emerging Images of
Aging in Gerontology," in ibid., 96.

10. See Andrea Charise, "'Let the Reader Think of the Burden': Old Age and the Crisis of Capacity," *Occasion* 4 (2012), http://occasion.stanford.edu/node/96.

11. Pat Thane, "The Twentieth Century," in *A History of Old Age,* ed. Pat Thane
(London: Thames & Hudson, 2005), 284.

12. On the Nuffield Foundation studies, see Simone de Beauvoir, *Old Age,* trans.
Patrick O'Brian (Harmondsworth: Penguin, 1970), 259; see also Harry R. Moody, *Aging:
Concepts and Controversies* (Thousand Oaks, CA: Pine Forge, 2000), 393.

13. Dan P. McAdams, "Explorations in Generativity in Later Years," in *Aging in the
Twenty-first Century: A Developmental Perspective,* ed. Len Sperry and Harry Prosen
(New York: Garland, 1996), 39; "grand-generative function" is the term used for the aged
in Erik H. Erikson, *The Life Cycle Completed,* extended version (New York: Norton,
1982), 63.

14. Kenneth Clark, *The Artist Grows Old* (Cambridge: Cambridge University Press,
1972), 21.

15. The rage theory (as either positive or negative) is shared by Leon Edel, "Portrait of
the Artist as an Old Man," in *Aging, Death and the Completion of Being,* ed. David D.
Van Tassel (Philadelphia: University of Pennsylvania Press, 1979, 212–13; the depressive
one, by Amir Cohen-Shalev, "Old Age Style: Developmental Changes in Creative Production from a Life-Span Perspective," *Journal of Aging Studies* 3 (1989): 33, and William
Kerrigan, "Life's Lamb: The Scansion of Late Creativity in the Culture of the Renaissance," in *Memory and Desire: Aging—Literature—Psychoanalysis,* ed. Murray M.
Schwartz and Kathleen Woodward (Bloomington: Indiana University Press, 1986), 171.

16. See, for example, Rudolph Arnheim, "On the Late Style of Life and Art," *Michigan Quarterly Review* 17 (1978): 149–50; and David Gervais, "Cézanne Early and Late,"
Cambridge Quarterly 13, no. 3 (1984): 205.

17. Edward W. Said, *On Late Style: Music and Literature Against the Grain* (New
York: Pantheon, 2006), 7.

18. Thomas Dormandy, *Old Masters: Great Artists in Old Age* (London and New
York: Hambledon & London, 2000), 217.

19. Clark, *The Artist Grows Old,* 19; the other position is that of, among others,
Hermann Broch, "The Style of the Mythic Age," introduction to Rachel Bespaloff, *On
the Iliad,* trans. Mary McCarthy (Washington, DC: Pantheon, 1947), 23.

20. Dean Keith Simonton, *Genius and Creativity: Selected Papers* (Greenwich:
Ablex, 1997), 227.

21. Beauvoir, *Old Age,* passim.

22. See Hans-Joachim von Kondratowitz, "The Medicalization of Old Age: Continuity and Change in Germany from the Late Eighteenth to the Early Twentieth Century,"

in *Life, Death and the Elderly: Historical Perspectives*, ed. Margaret Pelling and Richard M. Smith (London: Routledge, 1991), 134–64.

23. Margaret Morganroth Gullette, *Agewise: Fighting the New Ageism in America* (Chicago: University of Chicago Press, 2011), 165, passim.

24. See Tamara K. Hareven, "The Discovery of Old Age and the Social Construction of the Life Course," in *Images of Aging in Western Societies*, ed. Cornelia Hummel and Christian J. Lalive D'Epinay (Geneva: Centre for Interdisciplinary Gerontology, 1995), 18–23.

25. See Chris Phillipson, *Capitalism and the Construction of Old Age* (London: Macmillan, 1982); and Beauvoir, *Old Age*, 251–54.

26. Katz, *Disciplining*, 61.

27. Ibid., 117–18.

28. Vern L. Bengtson, Norella M. Putney, and Malcolm L. Johnson, "The Problem of Theory in Gerontology Today," in Johnson, Bengtson, Coleman, and Kirkwood, *The Cambridge Handbook of Age and Ageing*, 13.

29. See Elaine Cumming and William E. Henry, *Growing Old: The Process of Disengagement* (New York: Basic Books, 1961).

30. Katz, *Disciplining*, 125.

31. R. J. Manheimer, "Wisdom and Method: Philosophical Contributions to Gerontology," in *Handbook of the Humanities and Aging*, ed. Thomas R. Cole, David Dirck Van Tassel, and Robert Kastenbaum (New York: Springer, 1992), 428. See also B. W. Lemon, V. L. Bengtson, and J. A. Peterson, "An Exploration of the Activity Theory of Aging," *Journal of Gerontology* 27 (1972): 511–23.

32. See Lars Tornstam, "Gerotranscendence: A Theory about Maturing in Old Age," *Journal of Aging and Identity* 1 (1996): 37–50, and his subsequent book, *Gerotranscendence: A Developmental Theory of Positive Aging* (1874; New York: Springer, 2005).

33. G. M. Beard, *Legal Responsibility in Old Age* (New York: Russell, 1987); Adolphe Quételet, *A Treatise on Man and the Development of His Faculties* (Edinburgh: W. & R. Chambers, 1842); and Harvey Lehman, *Age and Achievement* (Princeton: Princeton University Press, 1953), 324.

34. Wayne Dennis, "Creative Productivity between the Ages of 20 and 80 Years," *Journal of Gerontology* 21 (1966): 1–8; and Dean Keith Simonton, *Genius, Creativity, and Leadership* (Cambridge: Cambridge University Press, 1984), 100.

35. Joseph Esposito, *The Obsolete Self: Philosophical Dimensions of Aging* (Berkeley and Los Angeles: University of California Press, 1987), 56.

36. Albert Einstein, "Opus Ultimum," *Musical Quarterly* 22 (1937): 269–86.

37. We have chosen to use this odd word "personhood" more often than the more usual and connected terms of "self," "identity," and "subjectivity" in an attempt to avoid the ideologically and professionally fraught baggage that goes with each.

38. Eric J. Cassell, *The Nature of Suffering and the Goals of Medicine* (New York: Oxford University Press, 2004), 160.

39. Ibid., 45.

40. Ibid., 41 and 42.

41. Today, personhood has come to be seen as a developmental process that is dynamic and ongoing throughout the life course. Various theoretical perspectives all inter-

pret it as a mixture of stability and flexibility, or "dynamic homeostasis." See Ursula M. Staudinger, "Personality and Aging," in Johnson, Bengtson, Coleman, and Kirkwood, *The Cambridge Handbook of Age and Ageing*, 239. In the past, the view was more likely to be one of a "core self, beset by difficulties and assaults to its integrity, that is *kept* stable over time" (Simon Biggs, *The Mature Imagination: Dynamics of Identity in Midlife and Beyond* [Buckingham: Open University Press, 1999], 48, emphasis in original).

42. Morris Rosenberg, *Conceiving the Self* (New York: Basic Books, 1979), 45–49.

43. Ibid., 34–37.

44. Quoted in Hans Busch, *Verdi's "Falstaff" in Letters and Contemporary Reviews* (Bloomington: Indiana University Press, 1997), 320.

45. See C. G. Jung, *Two Essays on Analytical Psychology*, trans. R. F. C. Hull (London: Routledge & Kegan Paul, 1953), 190; and Biggs, *The Mature Imagination*, 6.

46. We take it as given that this kind of construct is ideological, that the subject is both a social agent and a social construction. See Katz, *Disciplining*, 12.

47. McAdams, "Explorations," 39.

CHAPTER TWO

1. See Eric Crozier, "The Writing of *Billy Budd*," *Opera Quarterly* 4, no. 3 (1986): 23.

2. Nicholas Delbanco, *Lastingness: The Art of Old Age* (New York: Grand Central, 2011), 2.

3. Burton D. Fisher, *The Tales of Hoffmann ("Les Contes d'Hoffmann"): A French Opera in Three Acts with a Prologue and Epilogue; Music by Jacques Offenbach* (Miami: Opera Journeys, 2001), 11.

4. Anton Henseler, *Jakob Offenbach*, quoted in Heather Hadlock, *Mad Loves: Women and Music in Offenbach's "Les contes d'Hoffmann"* (Princeton: Princeton University Press, 2000), 86.

5. Fisher, *Tales of Hoffmann*, 15.

6. In Roger Nichols, ed., *Camille Saint-Saëns: On Music and Musicians* (Oxford: Oxford University Press, 2008), 155.

7. Letter to Hippolyte de Villemessant, 30 December 1860, quoted in Alain Decaux, *Offenbach: roi du Second Empire* (Paris: Pierre Amiot, 1958), 262.

8. Gabriel Grovlez, "Jacques Offenbach: A Centennial Sketch," *Musical Quarterly* 3 (1919): 337.

9. For an imagined account of the glittering cosmopolitan and aristocratic audience, see Sacheverell Sitwell, *La Vie Parisienne: A Tribute to Offenbach* (London: Faber & Faber, 1937), 26–40.

10. Decaux, *Offenbach*, 207.

11. Ibid., 208; see also James Harding, *Jacques Offenbach: A Biography* (London: John Calder; New York: Riverrun Press, 1980), 251: "The mood of the Second Empire chanced to be one that was cynical, even fatalistic. Offenbach expressed it admirably."

12. Decaux, *Offenbach*, 209.

13. See ibid., 215–28.

14. Arthur Moss and Evalyn Marvel, *Cancan and Barcarolle: The Life and Times of Jacques Offenbach* (Westport, CT: Greenwood Press, 1954), 259.

15. Ibid., 227.

16. Ibid., 262.

17. "Jacques Offenbach," *Neue freie Presse* (Vienna), translated and reprinted in *Musical World* 58, no. 44 (30 October 1880): 693–94.

18. Eduard Hanslick, quoted in Siegfried Kracauer, *Jacques Offenbach and the Paris of His Time*, trans. Gwenda Davis and Eric Moshbacher (New York: Zone, 2002), 346.

19. Hadlock, *Mad Loves*, 87.

20. Kracauer, *Jacques Offenbach*, 347; see also Decaux, *Offenbach*, 244, on the same theme.

21. Decaux, *Offenbach*, 250.

22. Victor W. Marshall, *Last Chapters: A Sociology of Aging and Dying* (Monterey, CA: Brooks/Cole, 1980), 107.

23. Quoted in Moss and Marvel, *Cancan*, 271.

24. For more on this, see Kimberley Fairbrother Canton, Amelia DeFalco, Linda Hutcheon, Michael Hutcheon, Katherine R. Larson, and Helmut Reichenbächer, "*Death in Venice* and Beyond: Benjamin Britten's Late Works," *University of Toronto Quarterly* 81, no. 4 (2012): 893–908.

25. *Musical Times* 21 (1 November 1880), 551.

26. Moss and Marvel, *Cancan*, 267.

27. Grovlez, "Jacques Offenbach," 333.

28. *Saturday Review* 50, 9 October 1880, 458.

29. Hanslick, "Jacques Offenbach," 692.

30. Fisher, *Tales of Hoffmann*, 16.

31. Anthony Edward Barone, "Richard Wagner's *Parsifal* and the Hermeneutics of Late Style" (Ph.D. diss., Columbia University, 1996), 132. The following discussion draws on Barone's fine historical and philosophical analysis.

32. See H. J. Schrimpf, *Goethe: Spätzeit, Altersstil, Zeitkritik* (Pfullingen: Neske, 1966).

33. For a more extensive discussion, see Linda Hutcheon and Michael Hutcheon, "Late Style(s): The Ageism of the Singular," *Occasion* 4 (2012). Accessed 20 November 2012, arcade.stanford.edu/journals/occasion.

34. Len Sperry, "Aging as a Developmental Process," in *Aging in the Twenty-first Century: A Developmental Perspective*, ed. Len Sperry and Harry Prosen (New York: Garland, 1996), 6. See also Blossom T. Wigdore, "Public Awareness of Aging: Its Impact," in *Images of Aging in Western Societies: Proceedings of the Second "Images of Aging" Conference*, ed. Cornelia Hummel and Christian J. Lalive d'Epinay (Geneva: Centre for Interdisciplinary Gerontology, 1995), 104.

35. Kenneth Clark, *The Artist Grows Old* (Cambridge: Cambridge University Press, 1972), 207.

36. See Georg Simmel, "Das Abendmahl Leonardo da Vincis," in Georg Simmel, *Zur Philosophie der Kunst: philosophische und kunstphilosophische Aufsätze*, ed. Gertrud Simmel (Potsdam: Kiepenheuer, 1922); Albert Erich Brinckmann, *Spätwerke grosser Meister* (Frankfurt a/M: Frankfurter Verlags-Anstalt, 1925); and Theodor W. Adorno, "Alienated Masterpiece: The *Missa Solemnis*" (1956), reprinted in *Telos* 28 (1976), 113–24.

37. Gordon McMullan, *Shakespeare and the Idea of Late Writing: Authorship in the Proximity of Death* (New York: Cambridge University Press, 2007), 5.

38. Barone, "Richard Wagner," 132ff.

39. Aside from the early failure of *Un giorno di regno*, composed during a period (1838–40) in which the composer suffered the death of his wife and children.

40. Respectively, see Julian Budden, *The Operas of Verdi*, vol. 3, *From "Don Carlos" to "Falstaff"* (Oxford: Clarendon Press, 1992), 295; and Renato Barilli, *Il paese del melodramma* (Lanciano: Carabba, 1930), as cited in James Hepokoski, *Giuseppe Verdi: "Falstaff"* (Cambridge: Cambridge University Press, 1983), 142.

41. An example of the positive reading of this looking-backward is that of Edward W. Said, *On Late Style: Music and Literature Against the Grain* (New York: Pantheon, 2006), 25–47; for the negative, see Norman Del Mar, *Richard Strauss: A Critical Commentary on His Life and Works*, vol. 2 (London: Barrie & Rockcliff, 1969), 199 and 225.

42. For more on this, see Barone, "Richard Wagner," 318.

43. Daniel Albright, introduction to *Modernism and Music: An Anthology of Sources*, ed. Daniel Albright (Chicago: University of Chicago Press, 2004), 11.

44. Richard Taruskin, *The Oxford History of Western Music*, vol. 4, *The Early Twentieth Century* (Oxford: Oxford University Press, 2005), 169.

45. Albright, introduction to *Modernism and Music*, 8.

46. Ibid., 20.

47. Ibid., 15.

48. Marcus Zagorski, "Material and History in the Aesthetics of 'serielle Musik,'" *Journal of the Royal Musical Association* 134, no. 2 (2009): 272.

49. See Linda Hutcheon and Michael Hutcheon, "One Saint in Eight Tableaux: The Untimely Modernity of Olivier Messiaen's *Saint François d'Assise*," in *Modernism and Opera*, ed. Richard Begam and Matthew Smith (Berkeley and Los Angeles: University of California Press, forthcoming).

CHAPTER THREE

1. Letter to Countess Maffei, 13 December 1863, in *Letters of Giuseppe Verdi*, ed. Charles Osborne (London: Victor Gollancz, 1971), 133.

2. For accounts of how deeply Verdi was hurt, see his letters cited in Julian Budden, *Verdi* (New York: Vintage, 1985), 90, and Mary Jane Phillips-Matz, *Verdi: A Biography* (Oxford: Oxford University Press, 1993), 469–70. That he continued to feel this way for years is attested to by Marcello Conati in his introduction to *The Verdi–Boito Correspondence*, ed. Marcello Conati and Mario Medici, trans. William Weaver (Chicago: University of Chicago Press, 1994), entitled "The Value of Time," xii–lxiv, passim.

3. See Mary-Lou Vetere, "Italian Opera from Verdi to Verismo: Boito and *La Scapigliatura*" (Ph.D. diss., SUNY Buffalo, 2010), 10 and 33–52. On the sense by the 1860s that Italian opera was losing its vitality, see Budden, *Verdi*, 34–5.

4. David C. Large and William Weber, introduction to *Wagnerism in European Culture and Politics*, ed. Large and Weber (Ithaca, NY: Cornell University Press, 1984), 16.

5. Marion S. Miller, "Wagnerism, Wagnerians, and Italian Identity," in Large and Weber, *Wagnerism*, 169–70, on the dissemination of Wagner's theories in Italy.

6. Letter from Charles Baudelaire to Richard Wagner, 17 February 1860, www
.planetewagner.net/lettre_de_charles_baudelaire.htm, accessed 19 November 2012.

7. David Kimbell, *Italian Opera* (Cambridge: Cambridge University Press, 1991), 541;
and Anselm Gerhard, *The Urbanization of Opera: Music Theater in Paris in the Nineteenth Century*, trans. Mary Whittall (Chicago: University of Chicago Press, 1998), 11.

8. See Alexandra Wilson, *The Puccini Problem: Opera, Nationalism and Modernity*
(Cambridge: Cambridge University Press, 2007), 14.

9. Peter Conrad, *Verdi and/or Wagner: Two Men, Two Worlds, Two Centuries* (London: Thames & Hudson, 2011). See also Timothée Picard, *Verdi–Wagner: Imaginaire de
l'opéra et identités nationales* (Rennes: Actes Sud, 2013).

10. Letter from Verdi to Giulio Ricordi, 20 April 1878, in *Verdi: The Man in His Letters*, ed. Franz Werfel and Paul Stefan, trans. Edward Downes (Freeport, NY: Books for
Libraries Press, 1970), 344–45.

11. See Tom Kington, "Italian Opera House Accused of Dealing 'a Blow for National Pride in a Moment of Crisis' by Going German for Its Season Opener," *Guardian*,
4 December 2012, http://www.guardian.co.uk/world/2012/dec/04/la-scala-wagner-verdi
-battle.

12. Phillips-Matz, *Verdi: A Biography*, 508.

13. Ibid., 568; Budden, *Verdi*, 104.

14. See Phillips-Matz, *Verdi: A Biography*, 284 (re: *Rigoletto*), 521 and 522 (re: *Don
Carlos*), 596 and 612 (re: *Aida*), and 674 (re: *Don Carlo*). See also comments by Bizet and
others quoted in Budden, *Verdi*, 96.

15. James A. Hepokoski, *Giuseppe Verdi: "Falstaff"* (Cambridge: Cambridge University Press, 1983), 85.

16. Quoted in Phillips-Matz, *Verdi: A Biography*, 669.

17. Quoted in ibid., 732.

18. Werfel and Stefan, *Verdi: The Man in His Letters*, 264.

19. Letter from Verdi to Boito, 26 April 1884, cited in Conati and Medici, *The Verdi–
Boito Correspondence*, 74.

20. Blanche Roosevelt, "Verdi: Milan and *Otello*," in *Verdi's "Otello" and "Simon
Boccanegra" in Letters and Documents*, ed. Hans Busch, vol. 2 (Oxford: Clarendon
Press, 1988), 725 and 727 respectively.

21. Camille Bellaigue, review of the premiere at La Scala on 1 March 1887, *Revue
des deux mondes* 80 (March–April 1887), 214–25, quoted in Busch, *Verdi's "Otello,"* 701.

22. Phillips-Matz, *Verdi: A Biography*, 680.

23. Antonio Fogazzaro, letter to Mrs. Starbuck, quoted in Kimbell, *Italian Opera*, 611.

24. See Budden, *Verdi*, 280 and 284. It is also true that Boito's libretto, with its
"metrical and formal fluidity" allowed for freer composition. See Kimbell, *Italian
Opera*, 606.

25. Osborne, *Letters*, 239–40.

26. Quoted in Hans Busch, ed., *Verdi's "Falstaff" in Letters and Contemporary
Reviews* (Bloomington: Indiana University Press, 1997), 7.

27. Letter from Verdi to Boito, 7 July 1889, in Conati and Medici, *The Verdi–Boito
Correspondence*, 139.

28. Letter from Verdi to Boito, 10 July 1889, in ibid., 143.

29. See Conati and Medici, *The Verdi–Boito Correspondence*, passim.

30. Verdi had only once before tried his hand at comedy, with his early failure, *Un giorno di regno*, written shortly after his wife and son died, though he claimed he had been looking for a comic libretto for years. See his letter to Giulio Ricordi, 16 August 1879, in Busch, *Verdi's "Falstaff,"* xxvi.

31. Roger Parker, *"Falstaff,"* in *New Grove Dictionary of Opera*, ed. Stanley Sadie (London: Macmillan, 1992), 2:111.

32. Letter from Verdi to Boito, 9 March 1890, in Conati and Medici, *The Verdi–Boito Correspondence*, 155.

33. Busch, *Verdi's "Falstaff,"* 97.

34. For an extensive discussion of the veracity of this claim, see Denise Gallo, "Re-patriating *Falstaff*: Boito, Verdi and Shakespeare (in Translation)," *Nineteenth-Century Music Review* 7, no. 2 (2010): 7–34.

35. Busch, *Verdi's "Falstaff,"* 107 n. 5.

36. To Maria Waldman, quoted in Osborne, *Letters*, 242. See also his letter to Boito of 1 January 1891, in Conati and Medici, *The Verdi–Boito Correspondence*: "Big Belly does not proceed: I am troubled and distracted . . . The very sad past months" (172).

37. Busch, *Verdi's "Falstaff,"* 109.

38. Letter from Verdi to Bülow, 14 April 1892, in Werfel and Stefan, *Verdi: The Man in His Letters*, 404.

39. Emanuele Senici, "Verdi's *Falstaff* at Italy's Fin de Siècle," *Musical Quarterly* 85, no. 2 (2001): 275.

40. T. Montefiore, quoted in Kimbell, *Italian Opera*, 616.

41. Osborne, *Letters*, 485; see also Parker, *"Falstaff,"* 117.

42. See Michael Rose, "A Lyric Comedy Unlike Any Other," in *Verdi: "Falstaff"* (London: Calder; New York: Riverrun Press, 1982), 13–15.

43. Busch, *Verdi's "Falstaff,"* 108.

44. Ibid., 107 n. 5.

45. Ibid., 355.

46. Spike Hughes, *Famous Verdi Operas: An Analytical Guide for the Opera-Goer and Armchair Listener* (London: Robert Hale, 1968), 485 and 487.

47. Hepokoski, *Giuseppe Verdi*, 86.

48. Bruno Barilli, *Il paese del melodramma* (1929), quoted in Hepokoski, *Giuseppe Verdi*, 142.

49. Camille Bellaigue, *Revue des deux mondes*, 1 May 1894, quoted in Busch, *Verdi's "Falstaff,"* 533.

50. Eduard Hanslick, "Memoires of Verdi and *Falstaff* in Rome," quoted in ibid., 523.

51. For a detailed argument, see Linda Hutcheon and Michael Hutcheon, "'Tutto nel mondo è burla': Rethinking Late Style in Verdi (and Wagner)," in *Verdi 2001*, ed. Fabrizio della Seta, Roberta Montemorra Marvin, and Marco Marica (Florence: Olschki, 2003), 905–28.

52. See Linda Hutcheon, *A Theory of Parody: The Teachings of Twentieth-Century Art Forms* (Urbana and Chicago: University of Illinois Press, 2000).

53. Michele Girardi, "French Sources of *Falstaff* and Some Aspects of Its Musical Dramaturgy," *Opera Quarterly* 11 (1995): 52; see also Hepokoski, *Giuseppe Verdi*, 86.

54. Budden, "Verdi," 105.

55. D. Cairns, "Full of Nimble, Fiery and Delectable Shapes," in *Verdi: "Falstaff"* (London: Calder; New York: Riverrun Press, 1982), 20.

56. Giuseppe Verdi, *Falstaff: Commedia lirica in tre atti*, libretto by Arrigo Boito, ed. Eduardo Rescigno (Milan: Ricordi, 1991), 148.

57. John Rosselli, *The Life of Verdi* (Cambridge: Cambridge University Press, 2000), 183.

58. Cited in ibid., 166.

59. Quoted in Busch, *Verdi's "Falstaff,"* 535.

60. See the anecdote about Anton Seidl in Caroline V. Kerr, ed. and trans., *The Bayreuth Letters of Richard Wagner* (Boston: Small, Maynard, 1912), 339. See also the extended discussion of Wagner's self-doubts in Anthony Barone, "Richard Wagner's *Parsifal* and the Hermeneutics of Late Style" (Ph.D. diss., Columbia University, 1996), 82, 89–93, 277, and 201.

61. Roger Parker, *Remaking the Song: Operatic Visions and Revisions from Handel to Berio* (Berkeley and Los Angeles: University of California Press, 2006), 85 and 84 respectively.

62. Barone, "Richard Wagner's *Parsifal*," 277.

63. For more on the relationship of the essays and the opera, see Theodor W. Adorno, *In Search of Wagner*, trans. R. Livingstone (London: Verso, 1981), 140; R. W. Gutman, *Richard Wagner: The Man, His Mind, and His Music* (1968; reprint, New York: Harcourt Brace Jovanovich, 1990), 421–40; and L. J. Rather, *Reading Wagner: A Study in the History of Ideas* (Baton Rouge: Louisiana State University Press, 1990), 284ff. Cf. Barry Millington, "*Parsifal*: A Work for Our Times," *Opera* 39 (1988): 14, and "*Parsifal*: A Wound Reopened," *Wagner* 8 (1987): 114.

64. Verdi, *Falstaff*, 74. All these citations are from this page, and the literal translations are ours.

65. Cairns, "Full," 27; Hughes, *Famous*, 496.

66. Verdi, *Falstaff*, 122.

67. Hughes, *Famous*, 510.

68. Ibid.; Budden, *The Operas*, 503.

69. Verdi, *Falstaff*, 122.

70. Parker, *Remaking the Song*, 76. Our reading of the comedy context and the libretto leads us to disagree with Parker's assessment of the Klingsor echo as "far from ironic" (87).

71. Verdi, *Falstaff*, 123, for all these citations.

72. Letter from Boito to Verdi, 19 March 1893, in Conati and Medici, *The Verdi–Boito Correspondence*, 205.

73. Letter from Verdi to Boito, 10 September 1891, in ibid., 188. He also tells his librettist that he is also adding a *"motive"* to be played by a solo violin in the catwalks over the stage: "Why not? If now they put orchestras in the cellar [as Wagner concealed the orchestra in Bayreuth], why couldn't we put a violin in the attic!!?" Parker sees this as a "troublesome" passage, left to the end for this reason (*Remaking the Song*, 72), but Verdi makes it clear in this letter that he did not see it in this way, though he did want to be sure that the opening recitative was "done carefully."

74. Verdi, *Falstaff*, 157.

75. Ibid., 157–58.

76. "Il fenomeno psicologico di Verdi," *La gazzetta musicale di Milano*, 5 March 1893, 159–60.

77. See Budden, *The Operas*, 447, 469–74, and 480–82 and passim.

78. Verdi, *Falstaff*, 74.

79. Quoted in Karen Henson, "Verdi versus Victor Maurel on *Falstaff*: Twelve New Verdi Letters and Other Operatic and Musical Theater Sources," *Nineteenth-Century Music* 31, no. 2 (2007): 129.

80. Letter from Verdi to Boito, 4 August 1898, in Conati and Medici, *The Verdi–Boito Correspondence*, 262.

81. Letter from Verdi to Teresa Stolz, quoted in Phillips-Matz, *Verdi: A Biography*, 759.

82. See letter from Verdi to Boito, 10 October 1897, in Conati and Medici, *The Verdi–Boito Correspondence*, 245.

83. Letter from Verdi to Giuseppe de Amicis [January 1901], quoted in Werfel and Stefan, *Verdi: The Man in His Letters*, 435–36.

84. For an extended analysis of Verdi's involvement in the Conservatory Reform Commission (and its 1871 Report) and of his last works as showing, rather than telling, his message, see Roberta Montemorra Marvin, *Verdi the Student—Verdi the Teacher* (Parma: Istituto Nazionale di Studi Verdiani, 2010), 57–93.

85. Letter from Boito to Verdi, October [1887], in Conati and Medici, *The Verdi–Boito Correspondence*, 123.

86. See, following on Erikson, Dan P. McAdams, "Explorations in Generativity in Later Years," in *Aging in the Twenty-first Century: A Developmental Perspective*, ed. Len Sperry and Harry Prosen (New York and London: Garland, 1996), 33–58.

87. Busch, *Verdi's "Falstaff,"* 467 n. 2. This was written following the success of *Falstaff* in Berlin in 1894.

88. Paul Kildea, *Benjamin Britten: A Life in the Twentieth Century* (London: Allen Lane, 2013), 282.

89. Wilson, *Puccini Problem*, 6.

CHAPTER FOUR

1. Journal of Romain Rolland, 1 March 1900, quoted in *Richard Strauss–Romain Rolland Correspondence*, ed. Rollo Myers (London: Calder & Boyars, 1968), 124–25.

2. For more on the conflicting biographies, see Kimberly F. Canton, Amelia De-Falco, Katherine R. Larson, and Helmut Reichenbächer, "Politics, Creativity, and the Aging Artist: Narrativising Richard Strauss's Last Years," *Life Writing* 6, no. 2 (2009): 211–27.

3. E.g., Norman Del Mar, *Richard Strauss: A Critical Commentary on His Life and Works* (London: Barrie and Rockcliff, 1962–72), 1:418.

4. E.g., Tim Ashley, *Richard Strauss* (London: Phaidon Press, 1999); George Richard Marek, *Richard Strauss: The Life of a Non-Hero* (London: Gollancz, 1967); and Michael Walter, *Richard Strauss und seine Zeit* (Laaber: Laaber Verlag, 2000), 348.

5. Ashley, *Richard Strauss*, 179–80; Heinrich Kralik, *Richard Strauss: Weltbürger der Musik* (Wollzeilen Verlag, 1963), 323; Michael Kennedy, *Richard Strauss: Man, Musician, Enigma* (Cambridge: Cambridge University Press, 1999), 318 and 354; and Charles Osborne, *The Complete Operas of Richard Strauss* (London: Michael O'Mara, 1988), 223–24.

6. Aubrey S. Garlington Jr., "Richard Strauss's *Vier letzte Lieder*: The Ultimate *opus ultimum*," *Musical Quarterly* 73, no. 1 (1989): 82. Others agree: Osborne, *Complete Operas*, 15; Del Mar, *Richard Strauss: A Critical Commentary*, 3:475, sees him as "almost mummified" in the pre-1914 musical world.

7. Quoted in Osborne, *Complete Operas*, 8.

8. "Richard Strauss. Born June 11, 1864," Part 2, trans. Samuel Weber and Shierry Weber, *Perspectives of New Music* 2 (1966): 114.

9. See appendix to Richard Strauss and Stefan Zweig, *A Confidential Matter: The Letters of Richard Strauss and Stefan Zweig, 1931–1935*, trans. Max Knight (Berkeley and Los Angeles: University of California Press, 1977), 108.

10. Marek, *Richard Strauss: The Life of a Non-Hero*, 15; see also Walter, *Richard Strauss und seine Zeit*, 348.

11. Strauss and Zweig, *A Confidential Matter*, 38. See, for a more negative take on this, Michael Meyer, *The Politics of Music in the Third Reich* (New York: Peter Lang, 1991), 109–10.

12. His letters to Zweig are clear on this; see also Kurt Wilhelm, *Richard Strauss: An Intimate Portrait* (London: Thames & Hudson, 1989), 9, 292. On his noninnocence, see Ashley, *Richard Strauss*, 10; in contrast to those who see him as naive (Ernst Krause, *Richard Strauss: The Man and His Work*, trans. John Coombs [London: Collet's, 1955], 66; Bryan Gilliam, *The Life of Richard Strauss* [Cambridge: Cambridge University Press, 1999], chapter 5), apolitical (Kralik, *Richard Strauss: Weltbürger der Musik*), or misguidedly political (Alan Jefferson, *Richard Strauss* [London: Macmillan, 1975], 51).

13. See Albrecht Riethmüller, "Stefan Zweig and the Fall of the Reich Music Chamber President, Richard Strauss," in *Music and Nazism: Art under Tyranny, 1933–1945*, ed. Michael H. Kater and Albrecht Riethmüller (Laaber: Laaber, 2003), 283.

14. Strauss and Zweig, *A Confidential Matter*, 99–100.

15. See Erik Levi, *Music in the Third Reich* (London: Macmillan, 1994), 217–18. It was his orchestral music that was the most performed, however; his operas were less popular in terms of numbers of productions than those of Wagner, Verdi, Puccini, Mozart, and Lortzing (192).

16. Strauss and Zweig, *A Confidential Matter*, 119.

17. Kennedy, *Richard Strauss: Man, Music, Enigma*, 293. For more on these years, see Michael Kater, *The Twisted Muse: Musicians and Their Music in the Third Reich* (New York: Oxford University Press, 1997), and especially Gerhard Splitt, *Richard Strauss, 1933–1935: Ästhetik und Musikpolitik zu Beginn der nationalsozialistischen Herrschaft* (Pfaffenweiler: Centaurus Verlagsgesellschaft, 1987).

18. Kennedy, *Richard Strauss: Man, Music, Enigma*, 292.

19. Ibid., 316.

20. Ibid., 173.

21. Ibid., 231.

22. Ibid., 216.

23. This is the negative view as summarized in ibid., 4—which he challenges in his very positive biography.

24. Del Mar, *Richard Strauss: A Critical Commentary*, 1:418. Del Mar, however, dates this decline from 1911 and blames Hofmannsthal for it.

25. Said, introduction to Donald Mitchell, *The Language of Modern Music* (London: Faber, 1993), 11.

26. Leon Botstein also sees an underlying aesthetic coherence in all Strauss's career; Botstein, "The Enigmas of Richard Strauss: A Revisionist View," in *Richard Strauss and His World*, ed. Bryan Gilliam (Princeton: Princeton University Press, 1992), 3–32. The same is true of Franz Grasberger, *Richard Strauss: Hohe Kunst, erfülltes Leben [mit Noten und Abbildungen]* (Vienna: Rosenbaum, 1965); and James L. Zychowicz, "The Late Operas of Richard Strauss," in *The Richard Strauss Companion*, ed. Mark-Daniel Schmid (Westport: Praeger, 2003), 293.

27. Garlington, "Richard Strauss's *Vier letzte Lieder*," 82–83.

28. Robert N. Butler, "The Life Review: An Interpretation of Reminiscence in the Aged," *Psychiatry* 26 (1963): 65–76.

29. David Murray, "Capriccio," in *New Grove Dictionary of Opera*, ed. Stanley Sadie (London: Macmillan, 1992), 1:721.

30. Kennedy, *Richard Strauss: Man, Music, Enigma*, 192.

31. Mozart's *Der Schauspieldirektor* (1786) and Salieri's *Prima la musica e poi le parole* (1786) are both on this theme.

32. Richard Strauss, *Capriccio: Ein Konversationsstück für Musik in einem Aufzug, Op. 85*, libretto by Clemens Krauss and Richard Strauss (Mainz: B. Schott's Söhne, 1942), 68. All translations here and elsewhere are our own literal ones.

33. Strauss, *Capriccio: Ein Konversationsstück*, 68 and 60 respectively.

34. Schuh, quoted in Ute Jung-Kaiser, "Zum 'musikalischen Testament' von Richard Strauss," in *Der kulturpädagogische Auftrag der Musik im 20. Jahrhundert*, ed. Ute Jung-Kaiser (Regensburg: Bosse, 1991), 100.

35. Strauss, *Capriccio: Ein Konversationsstück*, 31.

36. Ibid., respectively 20 and 36.

37. Murray, "Capriccio," 723.

38. See O. Erhardt, "The Later Operatic Works of Richard Strauss," *Tempo*, n.s., 12 (1949): 30; and Zychowicz, "The Late Operas," 294.

39. Jefferson, *Richard Strauss*, 82; Del Mar, *Richard Strauss: A Critical Commentary*, 1:177.

40. See Kennedy, *Richard Strauss: Man, Musician, Enigma*, 191; Del Mar, *Richard Strauss: A Critical Commentary*, 1:179; and Jefferson, *Richard Strauss*, 82.

41. Kennedy, *Richard Strauss: Man, Music, Enigma*, 241.

42. See Erhardt, "The Later Operatic Works," 30; Jung-Kaiser, "Zum 'musikalischen Testament," 109; and H. F. Redlich, "'Prima la musica . . . ?': A Ruminative Comment on Richard Strauss' Final Opera," *Music Review* 24 (1963): 189.

43. Del Mar, *Richard Strauss: A Critical Commentary*, 2:199 and 225.

44. See Kennedy, *Richard Strauss: Man, Music, Enigma*, 339; Matthew Boyden,

Richard Strauss (London: Weidenfeld & Nicolson, 1999), 340; and Jung-Kaiser, "Zum 'musikalischen Testament,'" 109.

45. We should, however, recall Strauss's admonitory words to Hofmannsthal after World War I: "[operatic] tragedy in the future, after this war, strikes me at present as rather idiotic and childish." Kennedy, *Richard Strauss: Man, Music, Enigma*, 194.

46. Willi Schuh, "Richard Strauss at Eighty," trans. Susan Gillespie, in Gilliam, *Richard Strauss and His World*, 293.

47. Walter Thomas, *Richard Strauss und seine Zeitgenossen* (Munich: A. Langen G. Müller, 1964), 333–34.

48. 15 September 1946, in Krause, *Richard Strauss: Gestalt und Werk*, 3rd ed. (1955; Leipzig: Breitkopf, 1983), 557. Nevertheless, in both 1945 and 1947 he suggested ideas to his librettist, Gregor, for new operas. None of these was ever actually composed. See Zychowicz, "The Late Operas," 297.

49. John Simon, "Testament," *Opera News* 62, no. 10 (31 January 1998): 8.

50. Strauss, *Capriccio: Ein Konversationsstück*, 82.

51. See Günther Brosche, ed., *Richard Strauss–Clemens Krauss: Briefwechsel Gesamtausgabe* (Tutzing: Hans Schneider, 1997), 240.

52. Ashley, *Richard Strauss*, 190; see also Jefferson, *Richard Strauss*, 102; and Redlich, "'Prima la musica,'" 188.

53. Kennedy, *Richard Strauss: Man, Music, Enigma*, 359; and Birgit Lodes, "Richard Strauss' Skizzen zu den 'Metamorphosen' und ihre Beziehung zu 'Trauer von München,'" *Die Musikforschung* 47, no. 3 (1994): 243 n. 22.

54. Kennedy, *Richard Strauss: Man, Music, Enigma*, 245.

55. Ibid., 359.

56. Boyden, *Richard Strauss*, 351.

57. Del Mar, *Richard Strauss: A Critical Commentary*, 3:412.

58. Kennedy, *Richard Strauss: Man, Music, Enigma*, 341.

59. For a full and revealing discussion of this attack, see Canton, DeFalco, Larson, and Reichenbächer, "Politics."

60. Ernest Krause, *Richard Strauss: Gestalt und Werk*, 419; Wilhelm, *Richard Strauss: An Intimate Portrait*, 267.

61. Many have noted references to *Tristan und Isolde*: Del Mar, *Richard Strauss: A Critical Commentary*, 3:437.

62. "Richard Strauss and the Question," in Gilliam, *Richard Strauss and His World*, 183. For him, it is "a belated and inadequate confrontation with self and history" (186).

63. Kennedy, *Richard Strauss: Man, Music, Enigma*, 427, 362.

64. Krause, *Richard Strauss: Gestalt und Werk*, 162.

65. Respectively, Kennedy, *Richard Strauss: Man, Musician, Enigma*, 193–94; Steinberg, "Richard Strauss," 182; and Adorno, "Richard Strauss," 124.

66. Krause, *Richard Strauss: Gestalt und Werk*, 458.

67. Klaus Mann, "Three German Masters," *Esquire* (January 1946): 198.

68. Timothy L. Jackson, "*Ruhe, meine Seele!* and the *Letzte Orchesterlieder*," in Gilliam, *Richard Strauss and His World*, 90.

69. Strauss to Schuh in 1943, quoted in Wilhelm, *Richard Strauss: An Intimate Portrait*, 257.

70. Krause, *Richard Strauss: Gestalt und Werk*, 424.

71. Michael Kater, *Musicians of the Nazi Era: Eight Portraits* (New York: Oxford University Press, 2000), 263.

72. Again, see Canton, DeFalco, Larson, and Reichenbächer, "Politics," for details.

73. Strauss quoted in Gilliam, *The Life*, 174 and Kennedy, *Richard Strauss: Man, Music, Enigma*, 361 (unpublished, from the Richard Strauss Archiv in Garmisch).

74. Boyden, *Richard Strauss*, 355; see also Jackson, *"Ruhe, meine Seele!,"* 200; and Wilfried Brennecke, "Die Metamorphosen-Werke von Richard Strauss und Paul Hindemith," *Schweizerische Musikzeitung* 103 (1963): 131.

75. Del Mar, *Richard Strauss: A Critical Commentary*, 3:469; and Susan Wanless, *Vier letzte Lieder: Four Last Songs* (Leeds: Mayflower, 1984), 51.

76. Boyden, *Richard Strauss*, 340.

77. Kennedy, *Richard Strauss: Man, Music, Enigma*, 382. While Strauss has been seen by Botstein as prefiguring postmodernism in his love of parody and ironic citation, if this is true the composer somehow skipped right over modernism.

78. Jung-Kaiser, "Zum 'musikalischen Testament,'" 95–98, on both the 1935 document and the later 1945 letter to Karl Böhm, in which he lists the works worthy of being in a "museum" of opera.

79. Schuh, "Richard Strauss at Eighty," 293.

80. Charles Youmans, "The Development of Richard Strauss's Worldview," in *The Richard Strauss Companion*, ed. Mark-Daniel Schmid (Westport: Praeger, 2003), 69.

81. For more on this, see Schuh, "Richard Strauss at Eighty," 288.

82. Ibid., 293.

83. Roth, quoted in Jackson, *"Ruhe, meine Seele!,"* 93.

84. Quoted in Kennedy, *Richard Strauss: Man, Music, Enigma*, 383.

85. As many have pointed out, Strauss worked on two other songs at this time. In June 1948 he orchestrated an earlier song, "Ruhe, meine Seele!," which would fit well with these four, and wrote another, "Malven," in November 1948 as a gift for the singer Maria Jeritza.

86. Respectively, Marek, *Richard Strauss: The Life of a Non-Hero*, 300; and Boyden, *Richard Strauss*, 346.

87. *Rosenkavalier* and *Ariadne auf Naxos*: see Jefferson, *Richard Strauss*, 91–92. *Guntram*: see Boyden, *Richard Strauss*, 364.

88. Jefferson, *Richard Strauss*, 956; Roland Tenschert, "Richard Strauss' Schwanengesang: Vier letzte Lieder für Sopran und Orchester," *Oesterreichische Musikzeitschrift* 5, nos. 10–11 (1950): 266.

89. Richard Strauss, *Vier letzte Lieder* (London: Boosey and Hawkes, 1950), 7–8.

90. Garlington, "Richard Strauss's *Vier letzte Lieder*," 90.

91. Strauss, *Vier letzte Lieder*, 31–32.

92. Ibid., 39–40.

93. Ibid., 47.

94. Ibid., 51–52.

95. Ibid., 53–54.

96. Del Mar, *Richard Strauss: A Critical Commentary*, 3:115.

97. Alan Jefferson, *The Lieder of Richard Strauss* (London: Cassell, 1971), 94.

98. Kennedy, *Richard Strauss: Man, Music, Enigma*, 386.

99. Jane Elizabeth Strickert, "Richard Strauss' *Vier letzte Lieder*: An Analytical Study" (Ann Arbor: UMI, 1975), iv.

100. Strauss, sadly, never heard the songs performed; they premiered in London in 1950.

101. Kennedy, *Richard Strauss: Man, Music, Enigma*, 118.

102. Quoted in Del Mar, *Richard Strauss: A Critical Commentary*, 1:78–79.

103. Rudolf Hartmann, "The Last Visit with Richard Strauss," trans. Susan Gillespie, in Gilliam, *Richard Strauss and His World*, 390.

CHAPTER FIVE

1. Quoted in Peter Hill and Nigel Simeone, *Messiaen* (New Haven: Yale University Press, 2005), 148.

2. Quoted in Père Jean-Rodolphe Kars, "The Works of Olivier Messiaen and the Catholic Liturgy," in *Olivier Messiaen: Music, Art, and Literature*, ed. Christopher Philip Dingle (Aldershot: Ashgate, 2007), 330.

3. Quoted in Hill and Simeone, *Messiaen*, 151.

4. See Stephen Broad, *Olivier Messiaen: Journalism, 1935–1939* (Farnham, Surrey: Ashgate, 2012).

5. Quoted, respectively, in Claude Samuel, *Olivier Messiaen: Music and Color; Conversations with Claude Samuel*, trans. E. Thomas Glasgow (Portland, OR: Amadeus Press, 1994), 231 and 21.

6. Andrew Shenton, "Messiaen's Theology," in *Olivier Messiaen's System of Signs: Notes towards Understanding His Music* (Aldershot: Ashgate, 2007), 18.

7. Marcel Delannoy, quoted in Hill and Simeone, *Messiaen*, 113.

8. Quoted in ibid., 147.

9. Messiaen, *Technique de mon langage musical* (Paris: Alphonse Leduc, 2000) 6; 93.

10. Quoted in Roger Nichols, "Messiaen at 70: Roger Nichols Talks to the Composer, Who Is 70 on December 10," *Music and Musicians* 27, no. 4 (December 1978): 20.

11. "Aggressive . . . gripping": Samuel, *Olivier Messiaen: Music and Color*, 168. "Émouvant": quoted in Hélène Cao, "Points de repère," in Olivier Messiaen, *Saint François d'Assise*, L'avant-scène opéra 223 (Paris: L'avant-scène opéra, 2004), 8.

12. Jean Boivin, *La classe de Messiaen* (Paris: Christian Bourgois, 1995), 98.

13. Christopher Dingle, *The Life of Messiaen* (Cambridge: Cambridge University Press, 2007), 151–52.

14. See Reginald Smith Brindle, *The New Music: The Avant-Garde since 1945* (London and New York: Oxford University Press, 1975), 9.

15. Messiaen, *Technique de mon langage*, 36.

16. Siglind Bruhn, *Messiaen's Interpretations of Holiness and Trinity: Echoes of Medieval Theology in the Oratorio, Organ Meditations, and Opera* (Hillodale, NY: Pendragon Press, 2008), 179.

17. François-Bernard Mâche, "Messiaen ornithologue," in *Olivier Messiaen: Le livre du centenaire*, ed. Anick Lesure and Claude Samuel (Paris: Perpetuum Mobile, 2008), 183.

18. "Introduction," in *The Messiaen Companion*, ed. Peter Hill (London: Faber & Faber, 2008), 8.

19. Conférence de Bruxelles, 1958; quoted in Malcolm Troup, "Orchestral Music of the 1950s and 1960s," in Hill, *The Messiaen Companion*, 395.

20. Alex Ross, *The Rest Is Noise: Listening to the Twentieth Century* (New York: Farrar, Straus & Giroux, 2007), 492.

21. In Claude Samuel, *Entretiens avec Olivier Messiaen* (Paris: Pierre Belfond, 1967), 59.

22. In ibid., 95.

23. Messiaen, *Technique de mon langage*, 36.

24. Dingle, *The Life of Messiaen*, 141.

25. Quoted in Paul Griffiths, *A Concise History of Modern Music from Debussy to Boulez* (London: Thames & Hudson, 1978), 137.

26. In Samuel, *Olivier Messiaen: Music and Color*, 249.

27. In Claude Samuel, *Conversations with Olivier Messiaen*, trans. Felix Aprahamian (London: Stainer & Bell, 1976), 82–3.

28. Quoted in Jean-Christophe Marti, "'It's a Secret of Love': An Interview with Olivier Messiaen [Jan. 1992]," trans. Stewart Spencer, reprinted in booklet, *Saint François d'Assise*, Hallé Orchestra; Kent Nagano, cond.; Dawn Upshaw, soprano; José van Dam, bass-baritone; Arnold Schoenberg Chorus; 4 discs (Deutsche Grammophon CD 445-776-2–445-780-2, 1999), 25.

29. In Samuel, *Conversations with Olivier Messiaen*, 82–83.

30. In Samuel, *Olivier Messiaen: Music and Color*, 208.

31. Dingle, *The Life of Messiaen*, 198.

32. Claude Samuel, *Permanences d'Olivier Messiaen: Dialogues et commentaires* (Arles: Actes sud, 1999), 415.

33. Seiji Ozawa, quoted in Lesure and Samuel, *Olivier Messiaen*, 71.

34. In Samuel, *Olivier Messiaen: Music and Color*, 215.

35. Daniel Mendelsohn, "The Truth Force at the Met," *New York Review of Books*, 12 June 2008, 24.

36. Theo Hirsbrunner, *Olivier Messiaen: Leben und Werk* (Laaber: Laaber-Verlag, 1988), 192.

37. In Samuel, *Olivier Messiaen: Music and Color*, 27, 209.

38. In ibid., 27.

39. Respectively, to Nagano in Orchestre Symphonique de Montréal, *Olivier Messiaen: Saint François d'Assise*, program book, December 2008, 41; and Samuel, *Olivier Messiaen: Music and Color*, 236.

40. Harry Halbreich, "Commentaire musical," in Messiaen, *Saint François d'Assise*, L'avant-scène opéra 223, 15; and Silvia Corbetta, *Olivier Messiaen: "Saint François d'Assise"; Cammino verso la joie parfaite* (Varese: Zecchini, 2009), 57.

41. Olivier Messiaen, *Saint François d'Assise (Scènes franciscaines): Opéra en 3 actes et 8 tableaux* (Paris: Éditions Musicales Alphonse Leduc, n.d.), 2:146–47. All translations from the French are our own literal ones.

42. Stefan Keym, *Farbe und Zeit: Untersuchungen zur musiktheatralen Struktur*

und Semantik von Olivier Messiaens "Saint François d'Assise" (Hildesheim: G. Olms, 2002), 63.

43. In Samuel, *Entretiens avec Olivier Messiaen*, 20.

44. Messiaen, *Saint François*, 4:1778–79.

45. Ross, *The Rest Is Noise*, 485.

46. Judith Crispin, "Introductory Note," in *Olivier Messiaen: The Centenary Papers* (Newcastle upon Tyne: Cambridge Scholars, 2010), xiv.

47. Samuel, *Olivier Messiaen: Music and Color*, 192.

48. In Brigitte Massin, *Olivier Messiaen: Une poétique du merveilleux* (Aix-en-Provence: Éditions Alinéa, 1989), 193.

49. Hill and Simeone, *Messiaen*, 224.

50. Quoted in ibid., 334.

51. Quoted in ibid., 340.

52. In Samuel, *Olivier Messiaen: Music and Color*, 249. The next citation is from the same page.

53. In ibid., 240.

54. Keym, *Farbe*, 179.

55. Ibid., 167.

56. In Samuel, *Olivier Messiaen: Music and Color*, 216.

57. In ibid., 27.

58. In ibid., 217.

59. Messiaen, *Saint François*, 1:3.

60. Ibid., 2:154.

61. Ibid., 2:181–82.

62. See Judith Crispin, "Messiaen's Transcendent Angels and the Ten *Duino Elegies* of Rilke," in Crispin, *Olivier Messiaen: The Centenary Papers*, 44–45.

63. "Piano Music II," in Hill, *The Messiaen Companion*, 326.

64. In Samuel, *Olivier Messiaen: Music and Color*, 94–95.

65. Quoted in Bruhn, *Messiaen's Interpretations*, 149 n. 2.

66. See Jean-Christophe Marti, "Rencontre avec Olivier Messiaen: 'J'ai subi et suivi une inspiration,'" in Messiaen, *Saint François d'Assise*, L'avant-scène opéra 223, 50.

67. In Samuel, *Olivier Messiaen: Music and Color*, 236.

68. "Orchestre d'angoisse," quoted in Reiner E. Moritz, "'Music and Poetry Have Brought Me into Thy Presence': Observations on Olivier Messiaen's *Saint François d'Assise*," liner notes, Messiaen, *Saint François d'Assise*, Hague Philharmonic Orchestra; Ingo Metzmacher, cond.; Camilla Tilling, soprano; Rodney Gilfry, baritone; Chorus of De Nederlandse Opera; Pierre Audi, dir.; 3 discs (Opus Arte DVD 1007, 2009), 11. "Savage harmonies . . . sound effects": ibid.

69. In Samuel, *Olivier Messiaen: Music and Color*, 241.

70. In ibid., 245.

71. Messiaen, *Saint François*, 4:133–34.

72. Ibid., 4:186–90.

73. Ibid., 4:263–67.

74. Keym, *Farbe*, 101.

75. Ibid., 29–31.

76. Richard Taruskin, *The Oxford History of Western Music* (New York: Oxford University Press, 2005), 4:235.

77. Philippe Albèra, "Le rythme repensé," in Lesure and Samuel, *Olivier Messiaen*, 96–97.

78. Wilfrid Mellers, "Mysticism and Theology," in Hill, *The Messiaen Companion*, 222; and Diane Luchese, "Olivier Messiaen's Slow Music: A Reflection of Eternity in Time," in Crispin, *Olivier Messiaen: The Centenary Papers*, 179–204.

79. Sander Van Maas, *The Reinvention of Religious Music: Olivier Messiaen's Breakthrough toward the Beyond* (New York: Fordham University Press, 2009), 158.

80. Annette Bossut, "Répétition et variation dans le livret *Saint François d'Assise* d'Olivier Messiaen," in *Musica e immagine: tra iconografia e mondo dell'opera* (Firenze: L. S. Olschki, 1993), 241.

81. Keym, *Farbe*, 201.

82. Messiaen, in Lesure and Samuel, *Olivier Messiaen*, 34, cited from *Traité de rythme, de couleur, et d'ornithologie* (Paris: A. Leduc, 1994–2002), 4:68–69.

83. Ross, *The Rest Is Noise*, 492.

84. See Marti, "Rencontre," 50.

85. In Samuel, *Olivier Messiaen: Music and Color*, 250.

86. See Paul Griffiths, *Olivier Messiaen and the Music of Time* (London: Faber, 1985), 241; Bruhn, *Messiaen's Interpretations*, 168–74; Keym, *Farbe*, 84; and David Palmer, "Messiaen's *Saint François d'Assise*," *Diapason* (May 1984): 6.

87. See Keym, *Farbe*, 84.

88. Halbreich, "Commentaire," 14.

89. Quoted in Lesure and Samuel, *Olivier Messiaen*, 77.

90. In ibid., 77.

91. In ibid., 78.

92. In ibid., 81.

93. In Samuel, *Olivier Messiaen: Music and Color*, 248.

94. See Michel Fischer, "Olivier Messiaen, *Saint François d'Assise (Scènes franciscaines)*: L'itinéraire musical d'un cheminement de la grâce," *Analyse musicale* 49 (December 2003): 47, 62.

95. In Lesure and Samuel, *Olivier Messiaen*, 78.

96. In ibid., 81.

97. In ibid., 78.

98. In Samuel, *Olivier Messiaen: Music and Color*, 248.

99. Philippe Olivier, in Lesure and Samuel, *Olivier Messiaen*, 78.

100. In Massin, *Olivier Messiaen*, 201.

101. Quoted in Hill and Simeone, *Messiaen*, 342.

102. In Massin, *Olivier Messiaen*, 201.

103. In ibid.

104. In Marti, "Rencontre," 58, emphasis added.

105. Hill and Simeone, *Messiaen*, 343–45.

106. Ibid., 350.

107. Quoted in Catherine Lechner-Reyaillet, *Messiaen: L'empreinte d'un géant* (Paris: Éditions Seguier, 2008), 223.

108. See, for both, Hill and Simeone, *Messiaen*, 353.

109. Ibid., 370.

110. Corbetta, *Olivier Messiaen: Cammino verso la joie parfaite*, 28.

111. Paul Griffiths, "Éclairs sur l'au-delà," in Hill, *The Messiaen Companion*, 510. The next two citations are on pp. 511 and 510 respectively.

112. Van Maas, *The Reinvention of Religious Music*, 145.

113. Ibid., 145–46.

114. Peter Hill, "Introduction," in Hill, *The Messiaen Companion*, 2.

115. In Marti, "Rencontre," 59.

116. In Pascal Arnault and Nicolas Darbon, *Messiaen: Les sons impalpables du rêve* (Lillebonne: Millénaire III Éditions, 1999), 5.

CHAPTER SIX

1. "*Awfully* frustrating": Britten to Peter Pears, 29 February 1968; Britten-Pears Library, The Red House, Aldeburgh, Suffolk (hereafter BPL). "Only a certain amount": Britten to William Plomer, 4 March 1968, in *Letters from a Life: The Selected Letters of Benjamin Britten, 1913–1976*, vol. 6, *1966–76*, ed. Philip Reed and Mervyn Cooke (Woodbridge, Suffolk: Boydell Press and Britten-Pears Foundation, 2012), 203.

2. Britten to William Plomer, 29 April 1968, in ibid., 216 and 217.

3. Respectively, the theses of Dr. Ian Tait, Britten's physician, as reported in Humphrey Carpenter, *Benjamin Britten: A Biography* (London: Faber & Faber, 1992), 542–43, and his surgeon Donald Ross, according to Dr. Hywel Davies, as reported in Paul Kildea, *Benjamin Britten: A Life in the Twentieth Century* (London: Allen Lane, 2012), 532ff.

4. We use the term *impairment* here in the sense that Disability Studies has come to use it to distinguish "'impairment' (an underlying biological or medical condition) from 'disability' (the meanings conferred on impairment by social and cultural construction)" (Joseph N. Straus, *Extraordinary Measures: Disability in Music* [Oxford: Oxford University Press, 2011], 4). While, as we shall see, Britten did face disability as well, it was the physical impairment that contributed most to his sense of having "aged."

5. Carpenter, *Benjamin Britten: A Biography*, 349.

6. For an assessment of his pianistic skill when he was still alive, see Paul Hamburger, "The Pianist," in *Benjamin Britten: A Commentary on His Work from a Group of Specialists*, ed. Donald Mitchell and Hans Keller (London: Rockcliff, 1952), 314–18.

7. Kildea, *Benjamin Britten: A Life in the Twentieth Century*, 72 and 139.

8. Respectively, Auden, quoted in Carpenter, *Benjamin Britten: A Biography*, 67; and Donald Mitchell, "An Introduction," in *Benjamin Britten: "Death in Venice"* (Cambridge: Cambridge University Press, 1987), 15.

9. Tippett, quoted in Carpenter, *Benjamin Britten: A Biography*, 196.

10. Britten, quoted in Imogen Holst, *Britten* (New York: Thomas Y. Crowell, 1965), 52.

11. Carpenter, *Benjamin Britten: A Biography*, 150.

12. Michael Oliver, *Benjamin Britten* (London: Phaedon Press, 1996), 44; and Kildea, *Benjamin Britten: A Life in the Twentieth Century*, 243, 252, 261, 269. On the rapid success of the opera internationally, see Holst, *Britten*, 43.

13. 20 September 1971, in Reed and Cooke, *Letters from a Life*, 451.

14. 21 October 1972, in ibid., 528.

15. Carpenter, *Benjamin Britten: A Biography*, 546.

16. Interview with Ian Tait, 15 May 2007 at the Red House; see also Carpenter, *Benjamin Britten: A Biography*, 541–44.

17. Carpenter, *Benjamin Britten: A Biography*, 576.

18. See ibid., 562.

19. Beth Britten, *My Brother Benjamin* (Abbotsbrook: Kensal Press, 1986), 197–98.

20. Rosamund Strode, "Working for Benjamin Britten (II)," in *The Britten Companion*, ed. Christopher Palmer (London: Faber & Faber, 1984), 61.

21. Michael Kennedy, *Britten* (London: Dent, 1993), 260. Britten had written for the harp and the treble voice as early as 1942, however, in *A Ceremony of Carols*.

22. "After his operation, Britten often confessed to Mrs [Mary] Potter, though probably to few others, that he was profoundly depressed and that he found life hardly worth living. He fretted about his disability, hated to be dependent on others and bitterly regretted not being able to work at full stretch. Up to the time of his illness, he was pretty tough and very active." Alan Blyth, *Remembering Britten* (London: Hutchinson, 1981), 107.

23. Michael Bury, "Chronic Illness as Biographical Disruption," *Sociology of Health and Illness* 4, no. 2 (1982): 169; see also Christian Lalive d'Epinay, "Images of Aging in Autobiographical Narratives of the Elderly," in *Images of Aging in Western Societies*, ed. Cornelia Hummel and Christian J. Lalive D'Epinay (Geneva: Centre for Interdisciplinary Gerontology, 1995), 144–45.

24. Interview with Stephen Ralls, 30 April 2007; see also Peter Pears's remarks about Britten as a "working musician" in Tony Palmer, dir., *A Time There Was* (Isolde Films, London Weekend Television, and RM Productions Fernseh- und Filmgesellschaft mbH, 1979).

25. Britten to William Plomer, 29 July 1973, in Reed and Cooke, *Letters from a Life*, 581.

26. Barbara Britten to Britten, 30 October 1973, BPL.

27. E.g., Britten to Donald and Kathleen Mitchell, 29 June 1975, in Reed and Cooke, *Letters from a Life*, 684.

28. Britten, quoted in Kennedy, *Britten*, 104, and Carpenter, *Benjamin Britten: A Biography*, 570.

29. In Blyth, *Remembering Britten*, 59.

30. Oliver, *Benjamin Britten*, 119–20.

31. Kildea, *Benjamin Britten: A Life in the Twentieth Century*, 321, 350, 369–70, 386, 423, 446–48, and 459.

32. The biographies are full of other such anecdotes. Peter Pears tells of the composer's illness while in America: bedridden, he continued to write down musical ideas, filling a sketchbook with them. See Britten, *My Brother*, 132.

33. Oliver, *Benjamin Britten*, 80 and 98; see David Matthews, *Britten* (London: Haus Publishing, 2003), 13, for an account of composing in bed during a boyhood illness.

34. This is a recurring motif in both Carpenter's biography, *Benjamin Britten: A Biography*, 161, 271, 373, 444, 472, and 481; and Kildea, *Benjamin Britten: A Life in the Twentieth Century*, 225 and 321.

35. Arnold Whittall, *The Music of Britten and Tippett: Studies in Themes and Techniques* (New York: Cambridge University Press, 1982), 309.

36. See Carpenter, *Benjamin Britten: A Biography*, 554; see also Mitchell, "An Introduction," in Reed and Cooke, *Letters from a Life*, 24. Stephen Arthur Allen sees the final work, the *Welcome Ode*, as a "miniature summary of the compositional worlds of Britten's past" ("Britten and the World of the Child," in *Benjamin Britten*, ed. Mervyn Cooke [Cambridge: Cambridge University Press, 2011], 291).

37. Kennedy, *Britten*, 249; David Matthews, "Britten's Third Quartet," *Tempo*, n.s. 125 (1978): 21; and Robert Saxton, quoted in Carpenter, *Benjamin Britten: A Biography*, 590; Peter Evans, *The Music of Benjamin Britten* (Oxford: Clarendon Press, 1996), 348; and Kennedy, *Britten*, 266.

38. Evans, *The Music of Benjamin Britten*, 415.

39. Gottfried Benn, "Artists and Old Age," trans. Ernest Kaiser and Eithne Wilkins, in *Primal Vision: Selected Writings of Gottfried Benn*, ed. E. B. Ashton (London: Marion Boyars, 1976), 208.

40. This is emphasized in all the biographies and by Dr. Tait in his interview. See also his friendship with the Right Reverend Leslie Brown, Bishop of St. Edmondsbury and Ipswich, in those last years. For more, see Graham Elliot, *Benjamin Britten: The Spiritual Dimension* (Oxford: Oxford University Press, 2006).

41. The most extensive analysis of this can be found in Philip Brett, *Music and Sexuality in Britten: Selected Essays*, ed. George E. Haggerty (Berkeley and Los Angeles: University of California Press, 2006). See also Christopher Chowrimootoo, "Bourgeois Opera: *Death in Venice* and the Aesthetics of Sublimation," *Cambridge Opera Journal* 22, no. 2 (2011): 175–216; and J. P. E. Harper-Scott, "Made You Look! Children in *Salome* and *Death in Venice*," in *Benjamin Britten: New Perspectives on his Life and Work*, ed. Lucy Walker (Woodbridge: Boydell Press, 2009), 116–135. In particular, Claire Seymour explores the "presence of a homosexual dynamic in both the verbal and musical texts" (3) in *The Operas of Benjamin Britten: Expression and Evasion* (Woodbridge, Suffolk: Boydell Press, 2004).

42. John Bridcut, *Britten's Children* (London: Faber & Faber, 2006).

43. Brett, *Music and Sexuality in Britten*, 194; see also Kildea, *Benjamin Britten: A Life in the Twentieth Century*, 116–17.

44. Oliver, *Benjamin Britten*, 12; see also Kildea, *Benjamin Britten: A Life in the Twentieth Century*, 414.

45. Journal entry, quoted in Carpenter, *Benjamin Britten: A Biography*, 80; Neil Powell, *Benjamin Britten: A Life for Music* (New York: Random House, 2013), 106; and Oliver, *Benjamin Britten*, 30.

46. Britten's boyishness: Carpenter, *Benjamin Britten: A Biography*, 74–75; Oliver, *Benjamin Britten*, 25 and 120; and Kildea, *Benjamin Britten: A Life in the Twentieth*

Century, 9, 10, 31, and 112. "He really hates growing up": Marjorie Fass, quoted in Carpenter, *Benjamin Britten: A Biography*, 114–15.

47. Alan Bennett, *The Habit of Art* (New York: Faber & Faber, 2009), 69. The original letter reads: "Wherever you go you are and probably always will be surrounded by people who adore you, nurse you, and praise everything you do, e.g. Elisabeth, Peter. . . . Up to a certain point this is fine for you, but beware. You see, Bengy dear, you are always tempted to make things too easy for yourself in this way, i.e. to build yourself a warm nest of love (of course when you get it, you find it a little stifling) by playing the lovable talented little boy." 31 January 1942, in Reed and Cooke, *Letters from a Life*, 2:1015–16. Also quoted in Carpenter, *Benjamin Britten: A Biography*, 164.

48. Bennett, *The Habit of Art*, 23.

49. See Carpenter, *Benjamin Britten: A Biography*, 347.

50. Oliver, *Benjamin Britten*, 71.

51. Quoted in Carpenter, *Benjamin Britten: A Biography*, 123.

52. Ibid., 262, 263, 315, 424, and 484–85; Oliver, *Benjamin Britten*, 25; Bridcut, *Britten's Children*, 1 and 19; and Kildea, *Benjamin Britten: A Life in the Twentieth Century*, 36. Amusingly, even his prose style has been described as "a sturdy, knockabout style befitting an intelligent public-school boy" in Paul Kildea, "Introduction," in *Britten on Music*, ed. Paul Kildea (Oxford: Oxford University Press, 2003), 3. But school was constructed less as a "haven" (as Kildea claims in "Britten, Auden and 'Otherness,'" in *The Cambridge Companion to Benjamin Britten*, ed. Mervyn Cooke [Cambridge: Cambridge University Press, 1999], 44), than as a symbol of youth.

53. Quoted in Bridcut, *Britten's Children*, 176.

54. "Boyishness as Much as Boys," review of John Bridcut, *Britten's Children*, *Telegraph*, 13 June 2006, http://www.telegraph.co.uk/culture/books/3653043/Boyishness-as-much-as-boys.html. Accessed 10 July 2012.

55. Oliver, *Benjamin Britten*, 51.

56. Allen, "Britten and the World of the Child," 291. See also Holst, *Britten*, 279.

57. See Michael Wilcox, *Benjamin Britten's Operas* (Bath: Absolute Press, 1997), 45–56 and 75–76.

58. Quoted in Bridcut, *Britten's Children*, 240.

59. Eric Crozier, quoted in Carpenter, *Benjamin Britten: A Biography*, 344.

60. Bridcut, *Britten's Children*, 5; see also Brett, *Music and Sexuality in Britten*, 24; and Kildea, *Benjamin Britten: A Life in the Twentieth Century*, 404–5. Indeed, Mildred Cary entitles her book *Benjamin Britten et le mythe de l'enfance* (Paris: Buchet/Chastel, 2006).

61. See Dan P. McAdams, "The Psychology of Life Stories," *Review of General Psychology* 5, no. 2 (2001): 106.

62. Wilcox, *Benjamin Britten's Operas*, 15.

63. Carpenter, *Benjamin Britten: A Biography*, 420.

64. Ibid., 421.

65. John Culshaw, "'Ben'—A Tribute to Benjamin Britten," in Palmer, *The Britten Companion*, 63. Palmer feels that the source of Britten's personal and professional insecurity was his double isolation: as a child in an adult world and as a homosexual in a heterosexual society. See "The Ceremony of Innocence," in Palmer, *The Britten Com-*

panion, 70. See also Kildea, *Benjamin Britten: A Life in the Twentieth Century*, 516–17.

66. Respectively, by William Mann in *The Times*, and Desmond Shawe-Taylor in the *Sunday Times*; quoted in Carpenter, *Benjamin Britten: A Biography*, 519.

67. Britten to Graham Johnston; see ibid., 476.

68. Quoted in ibid., 473.

69. Ibid., 569 and 584.

70. Donald Mitchell, quoted in ibid., 577, and Kildea, *Benjamin Britten: A Life in the Twentieth Century*, 553.

71. Myfanwy Piper, librettist, *Death in Venice: An Opera in Two Acts, Set to Music by Benjamin Britten* (London: Faber Music, 1973), 1.

72. Sandra Corse and Larry Corse, "Britten's *Death in Venice*: Literary and Musical Structures," *Musical Quarterly* 73 (1989): 345. For a detailed (Freudian) reading of this opening monologue and its musical and verbal representation of creative block, see Shersten Johnson, "At a Loss for Words: Writer's Block in Britten's *Death in Venice*," *PsyArt* (3 March 2008), http://www.psyartjournal.com/article/show/johnson-at_a_loss _for_words_writers_block_in_brittens_death_in_venice. Accessed 11 August 2012.

73. Kildea, *Benjamin Britten: A Life in the Twentieth Century*, 535.

74. Piper, *Death in Venice: An Opera in Two Acts*, 1.

75. Ibid.

76. Ibid., 3.

77. Ibid., 9.

78. Ibid., 9–10.

79. Quoted in Carpenter, *Benjamin Britten: A Biography*, 163–4; and Oliver, *Benjamin Britten*, 92–3.

80. Piper, *Death in Venice: An Opera in Two Acts*, 1.

81. Ibid., 8.

82. Ibid., 5.

83. Ibid., 34–35.

84. Carpenter is clear that Britten always rejected the foppish stereotype of gay male behavior, in part because of his desire to play it safe and be part of the establishment (*Benjamin Britten: A Biography*, 327). See also Bridcut, *Britten's Children*, 266–7, and Kildea, *Benjamin Britten: A Life in the Twentieth Century*, 536.

85. Allen, "Britten and the World of the Child," 279. See also Linda Hutcheon and Michael Hutcheon, *Bodily Charm: Living Opera* (Lincoln: University of Nebraska Press, 2000), 30–36 and 48–52.

86. Respectively, Brett, *Music and Sexuality in Britten*, 149; and Hutcheon and Hutcheon, *Bodily Charm*, 35.

87. Kildea, *Benjamin Britten: A Life in the Twentieth Century*, 530.

88. See Donald Mitchell, "What Do We Know about Britten Now?" in Palmer, *The Britten Companion*, 37. Mitchell summarizes Britten's position on modernism: "For it is clear now that he did not unswervingly pursue some compromised road of orthodoxy but on the contrary ruthlessly and comprehensively ransacked past and present, orthodox and unorthodox, fashionable and unfashionable, traditional and innovative, and took whatever was useful to him" (32).

89. BBC/ Decca DVD 074 3861.

90. See Paula B. Balber, "Stories of the Living-Dying: The Hermes Listener," in Inge B. Corless, Barbara B. Germino, and Mary A. Pittman, eds., *Dying, Death, and Bereavement: A Challenge for Living* (New York: Springer, 2006), 124, for more on the possible functions of these narratives.

91. C. F. Pond, "Benjamin Britten and T. S. Eliot: *Entre Deux Guerres* and After," in *T. S. Eliot's Orchestra: Critical Essays on Poetry and Music* (New York and London: Garland, 2000), 232.

92. Kennedy, *Britten*, 262. See also Evans on the "macabre nonchalance of the poem's last line" and the "sublime valedictory music" of the finale (*The Music of Benjamin Britten*, 449).

93. Respectively, Matthews, *Britten*, 150; and Kildea, *Benjamin Britten: A Life in the Twentieth Century*, 550.

94. Evans, *The Music of Benjamin Britten*, 396.

95. Kennedy, *Britten*, 264.

96. Oliver, *Benjamin Britten*, 207.

97. Quoted in Carpenter, *Benjamin Britten: A Biography*, 571.

98. Quoted in ibid., 563.

99. Thomson, quoted in ibid., 565.

100. McAdams, "The Psychology of Life Stories," 113, cites B. R. Josephson, J. A. Singer, and P. Salovey, "Mood Regulation and Memory: Repairing Sad Moods with Happy Memories," *Cognition and Emotion* 10 (1996): 437–44.

101. Kildea, *Benjamin Britten: A Life in the Twentieth Century*, 551.

102. Kennedy, *Britten*, 261.

103. Frances Sinclair, "Celebration of Youth and Innocence: Benjamin Britten's Welcome Ode," *Choral Journal* 39, no. 10 (1999): 11.

104. Sinclair, "Celebration," 12.

105. Many letters attest to this; see also Ronald Duncan, *Working with Britten: A Personal Memoir* (Welcombe: The Rebel Press, 1981), 156: "just before he died [Britten] had busied himself completing the purchase of the hotel on the front at Aldeburgh so that it could be used as an office for the Festival."

106. Oliver, *Benjamin Britten*, 210.

107. Quoted in Matthews, *Britten*, 155.

108. Beth Britten, *My Brother*, 199. See also Imogen Holst who kept a diary when she began working for Britten in 1952. On her first evening at Aldeburgh she wrote: "We were talking about old age and he said that he had a very strong feeling that people died at the right moment, and that the greatness of a person included the time when he was born and the time he endured, but that this was difficult to understand" (Imogen Holst, "Working for Benjamin Britten [I]," in Palmer, *The Britten Companion*, 50).

109. Quoted in Carpenter, *Benjamin Britten: A Biography*, 580. Britten himself felt that, with serial musical modernism in fashion, the universities and conservatories would not be interested in his work, in part because his "methods, which are entirely personal to me, are founded on a time when the language was not so broken as it is now." In Kildea, *Britten on Music*, 327, and *Benjamin Britten: A Life in the Twentieth Century*, 463.

110. McAdams is clear that life stories must develop and change over the life course ("The Psychology of Life Stories," 106).

111. The best summary of Baltes's theory is in Paul B. Baltes, Alexandra M. Freund, and Shu-Chen Li, "The Psychological Science of Human Aging," in *The Cambridge Handbook of Age and Ageing*, ed. Malcolm L. Johnson, Vern L. Bengtson, Peter G. Coleman, and Thomas B. L. Kirkwood (Cambridge: Cambridge University Press, 2005), especially 53–55.

112. See Johannes J. F. Schroots, "Theoretical Developments in the Psychology of Aging," *Gerontologist* 36, no. 6 (1996): 745.

113. Oliver, *Benjamin Britten*, 207.

114. Kildea, *Benjamin Britten: A Life in the Twentieth Century*, 557. See also 431, 458, 472, and 479.

115. Ibid., 557.

116. "The Ceremony of Innocence," 68.

117. Ibid., 82.

CHAPTER SEVEN

1. In Simon Morrison, *The People's Artist: Prokofiev's Soviet Years* (Oxford: Oxford University Press, 2009), 357.

2. Ibid., 339.

3. Ibid., 341.

4. Ibid., 348, 375, and 392.

5. Michael Beckerman, "Leoš Janáček and 'The Late Style' in Music," *Gerontologist* 30, no. 5 (1990): 634–36.

6. Ibid., 634.

7. Ursula M. Staudinger, "Personality and Aging," in *The Cambridge Handbook of Age and Ageing*, ed. Malcolm L. Johnson, Vern L. Bengtson, Peter G. Coleman, and Thomas B. L. Kirkwood (Cambridge: University of Cambridge Press, 2005), 240.

8. Victor Marshall, "The Micro-Macro Link in the Sociology of Aging," in *Images of Aging in Western Societies*, ed. Cornelia Hummel and Christian J. Lalive d'Epinay (Geneva: Centre for Interdisciplinary Gerontology, 1995), 355.

9. Michael Millgate, *Testamentary Acts: Browning, Tennyson, James, Hardy* (Oxford: Clarendon Press; New York: Oxford University Press, 1992), 1–2. See also Lawrence Lipking, *The Life of the Poet: Beginning and Ending Poetic Careers* (Chicago: University of Chicago Press, 1981), 72.

10. Roger Nichols, "Messiaen at 70," *Music and Musicians* 27, no. 4 (December 1978): 20.

11. Hans Werner Henze, *Bohemian Fifths: An Autobiography*, trans. Stewart Spencer (London: Faber & Faber, 1998), 483.

12. Rupert Christiansen, "Seduced by an Old Master," *Telegraph*, 18 August 2003, http://www.telegraph.co.uk/culture/music/classicalmusic/3600/93/Seduced-by-an-old -master.html. Accessed 13 January 2013.

13. David Clarke, *The Music and Thought of Michael Tippett: Modern Times and Metaphysics* (Cambridge: Cambridge University Press, 2001), 207.

14. See Sam Jordison, "Lawrence Durrell and Peggy Glanville-Hicks: A Song for Sappho," *Guardian*, 22 August 2012. http://www.guardian.co.uk/music/2012/aug/22/lawrence-durrell-glanville-hicks-sappho. Accessed 12 January 2013.

15. See Victoria Rogers, *The Music of Peggy Glanville-Hicks* (Burlington, VT: Ashgate, 2009), 239–40.

16. Quoted in Glenda Dawn Goss, *Jean Sibelius and Olin Downes: Music, Friendship, Criticism* (Boston: Northeastern University Press, 1995), 88.

17. "Jean Sibelius—the Website," http://www.sibelius.fi/english/elamankaari/sib_suosion_huipulla.htm. Accessed 11 April 2014.

18. Santeri Levas, *Jean Sibelius: A Personal Portrait*, trans. Percy M. Young (Porvoo: Werner Söderström Osakeyhtiö, 1972), 92–96.

19. Olin Downes, quoted in Nicholas Slonimsky, *Lexicon of Musical Invective: Critical Assaults on Composers since Beethoven's Time*, 2nd ed. (New York: Coleman-Ross, 1965), 161.

20. Originally published in the *Zeitschrift für Sozialforschung* in 1938, translated by Susan H. Gillespie as "Gloss on Sibelius," in *Jean Sibelius and His World*, ed. Daniel M. Grimley (Princeton: Princeton University Press, 2011), 335.

21. Tomi Mäkelä, *Jean Sibelius*, trans. Steven Lindberg (Woodbridge, Suffolk: Boydell Press, 2011), 239.

22. Tomi Mäkelä, "The Wings of a Butterfly: Sibelius and the Problems of Musical Modernity," in Gimley, *Jean Sibelius and His World*, 97.

23. Levas, *Jean Sibelius: A Personal Portrait*, 103.

24. Quoted in Mäkelä, *Jean Sibelius*, 391.

25. Leon Botstein, "Old Masters: Jean Sibelius and Richard Strauss in the Twentieth Century," in Grimley, *Jean Sibelius and His World*, 258.

26. Amy Fiske and Randi S. Jones, "Depression," in Johnson, Bengtson, Coleman, and Kirkwood, *The Cambridge Handbook of Age and Ageing*, 246.

27. Elliott Jaques, "Death and the Mid-Life Crisis," *International Journal of Psycho-Analysis* 46 (1965): 502–15.

28. Ibid., 506.

29. E-mail to authors, 19 January 2013.

30. Elizabeth Wood, "On Deafness and Musical Creativity: The Case of Ethel Smyth," *Musical Quarterly* 92, nos. 1–2 (2009): 33–69.

31. Smyth, letter to Alice Davidson, 27 March 1919. Quoted in Wood, "On Deafness," 35.

32. Wood, "On Deafness," 50.

33. Ibid., 41.

34. Smyth's diary, 6 November 1926. Quoted in Wood, "On Deafness," 60.

35. Quoted in Christopher St. John, *Ethel Smyth: A Biography* (London and New York: Longmans, Green, 1959), 239.

36. Constance Rooke, "Oh What a Paradise It Seems: John Cheever's Swan Song," in *Aging and Gender in Literature: Studies in Creativity*, ed. Anne M. Wyatt-Brown and Janice Rossen (Charlottesville: University Press of Virginia, 1993), 208.

37. Beckerman, "Leoš Janáček," 634.

38. Anthony Edward Barone, "Richard Wagner's *Parsifal* and the Hermeneutics of Late Style" (Ph.D. diss., Columbia University, 1996), 40ff.

39. Andrew Achenbaum, "Images of Old Age in America, 1790–1970: A Vision and a Re-Vision," in *Images of Aging: Cultural Representations of Later Life*, ed. Mike Featherstone and Andrew Wernick (London and New York: Routledge, 1995), 23.

40. See Kenneth Clark, *The Artist Grows Old* (Cambridge: Cambridge University Press, 1972), 21–22; Brinckmann, *Spätwerke grosser Meister* (Frankfurt am Main: Frankfurter Verlags-Anstalt, 1925), 18; and David Grene, *Reality and the Heroic Pattern: Last Plays of Ibsen, Shakespeare, and Sophocles* (Chicago: University of Chicago Press, 1967), vii.

INDEX